To Caroline, 1998.
Happy Christmas,
lots of love Tim & Mary
xxx

Catherine Reilly

Catherine Reilly was born in Stretford and educated in Manchester. She is a professional librarian, now retired, and is a Fellow of the Library Association and holds a M.Litt. from Oxford University. *Scars Upon My Heart* and *Chaos of the Night* were the first two of three women's poetry anthologies she has compiled, the most recent being *Winged Words* (Enitharmon Press 1994), a collection of Victorian poetry. She is also the author of *Late Victorian Poetry* (Mansell 1994) and major bibliographies of the poetry of the First and Second World Wars.

The Virago Book of Women's War Poetry and Verse

AN OMNIBUS EDITION OF **SCARS UPON MY HEART** AND **CHAOS OF THE NIGHT**

Edited and with a new introduction by
CATHERINE REILLY

To the memory of
Mary Schwarz
1924–1996

A *Virago* book

Published by Virago Press 1997

First published in Great Britain by Virago Press as two volumes: *Scars upon my Heart: Women's Poetry and Verse of the First World War* (1981) and *Chaos of the Night: Women's Poetry and Verse of the Second World War* (1984)

A CIP catalogue record for this book is available from the British Library

ISBN 1 86049 362 9

Printed and bound in Great Britain by Clays Ltd, St Ives plc

Virago
A Division of
Little, Brown and Company (UK)
Brettenham House
Lancaster Place
London WC2E 7EN

Contents

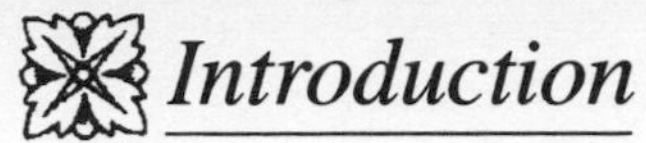

Introduction

Scars Upon My Heart (1981) and its companion volume *Chaos of the Night* (1984) are both by-products of my bibliographical research into the poetry and verse of the First and Second World Wars. The poetry of the Second World War has not yet attracted as much literary and critical attention as that of the First World War. Those who have studied the poetry of both wars have recognized that the first war produced some outstanding poetry by a relatively small number of poets, while the second war produced a great deal more good poetry.

Women's writing in general tended to be undeservedly neglected until Virago Press and other feminist publishing houses made available a large corpus of meritorious but little-known work by women. Until then anthologies of the poetry of both wars had been published over the years but the contributions were largely by men. The term 'war poet' was applied initially to the soldiers fighting in the trenches of France and Flanders. These anthologies often included poetry by such well-established literary lions as Thomas Hardy, Rudyard Kipling, D.H. Lawrence and W.B. Yeats, all non-combatants. So it appeared that the business of war was still regarded as primarily a masculine concern, even though women would have an increasingly active part to play in twentieth-century warfare.

The First World War left a deep scar in British national consciousness, a scar which exists even today in the minds of those belonging to the generations born since the war ended. What makes the poetry of this war so remarkable is that most of it is essentially poetry of protest against war, a protest made by citizens of a country with a long and proud military tradition. Never before in British history had war appeared other than heroic and glorious so publicly. After the tragic and senseless slaughter at Mons and the successive battles on the Somme, the loss of life at the front was such that hardly a family in the land was untouched by personal grief. In the future war poetry was less likely to be couched in heroic or romantic terms.

Literature, perhaps especially poetry, mirrors the society from which it springs. Although barely twenty-one years separate the two wars, the social and economic changes in British society during that time were enormous. People's attitude to war had changed: the disillusionment engendered during the years 1914–18 and those that followed ensured that there was no glorification of war or false patriotism in 1939, just a calm acceptance of the task ahead. As danger from enemy action by aerial bombardment was a shared fear, the gulf that had existed between soldier and civilian in the early years of the First World War became virtually non-existent this time.

In the inter-war years the position of women had also changed considerably. The campaign for women's suffrage had been successful, and by 1928 women over the age of twenty-one had the vote. An increasing number held jobs outside their homes, including that generation of women who had never married because the men they might have married had been killed on the Western Front. Women had proved their worth by working for victory in the First World War, and it was assumed that their role in the Second World War would be an even more vital and important one. The conscription of women was introduced in December 1941, with certain exemptions, and in practice extended to those aged nineteen to twenty-four. Women were liable to be called up for the women's auxiliary services, civil defence and essential civilian employment such as work in aircraft factories or on the land.

The poetry and verse in both collections will come as a surprise to many readers, demonstrating as they do a distinctive and positive 'women's voice'. It is tempting to draw parallels between the poetry of the two wars and indeed there are many similarities. Apart from significant social comment on these periods of twentieth-century history, a strong sense of war's realities is expressed. There is compassion, sympathy and honest responses of indignation and pity from women, some of whom had seen a little of the 'real thing' and were deeply moved by it. Women always excel when writing about human emotions and many poems here are concerned with the emotional upheaval caused by war and its attendant partings, separations and bereavements. The view of 'the women at home', ignorant and idealistic, was quite false. Women such as Mary Gabrielle Collins, S. Gertrude Ford, May Herschel-Clark and Winifred M. Letts were writing protest poetry before Wilfred Owen and Siegfried Sassoon. It was of course easier for women, not eligible for active service, to adopt an anti-war stance.

An anthologist has a duty to bring together as many facets of the subject as may be found. In a sense, any war poem is a statement against war. In both collections I have tried to present a wide range of topic and of literary style. The poems speak for themselves, demonstrating what women thought and felt about the wars, both at the time and in retrospect; they are a vivid yet sensitive record of a critical period in our history. Here, as elsewhere, 'the poetry is in the pity'.

Catherine W. Reilly, Cheshire 1997

Scars upon my Heart

Your battle-wounds are scars upon my heart,
Received when in that grand and tragic 'show'
You played your part
Two years ago . . .

VERA BRITTAIN

Contents

Preface by Judith Kazantzis

To read this book through from cover to cover is an extraordinary experience – and one I would suggest as a best first way to grasp the historical tragedy that lies behind these poems.

The voices of despair and endurance and anger are quiet, yet they mount steadily into a cumulative effect. Always behind them I am aware of the fraught gigantic backdrop of the War, the reality of 'The Shadow' of Rose Macaulay's poem. Against this looming 'Fear' and 'Pain' and 'Hell', where the young men are submerged, the woman's voice, as Catherine Reilly names it, becomes a tragic one, in several senses. From her uneasy position on the 'Rim of the shadow of the Hell' Rose Macaulay speaks sometimes with angry brilliance, sometimes with grateful idealism; there sounds under both a plain forlorn note.

We know of the male agony of the trenches from the poetry of soldiers like Sassoon and Owen. We know little in poetry of what that agony and its millions of deaths meant to the millions of English women who had to endure them – to learn to survive survival. This anthology fills a poignant gap. Just as the soldier poets with their personal experience of the fighting came to speak for a 'lost generation', so, much more modestly yet still truly, these women poets speak for the women whose own lives were often blighted by that miserable loss.

The war divided women and men not only by death: sad irony. Sweepingly Sassoon attacked women's romantic ignorance of its real nature in his piece 'Glory of Women': 'You love us when we're heroes, home on leave, / Or wounded in a mentionable place. . . .' The Jingo woman, answering Julian Grenfell, the warrior poet, may see the war partly as a holy rite, partly with maternal indulgence as a jolly game for the boys; but most poets here understand that war is no game, and they feel the insidious gulf between those who fought and those who waited – helpless to help the helpless.

So here is a part answer over many years to that soldiers' bitterness. As a representative voice it varies widely in poetic form, in skill and in argument. But horror of war pervades it.

After all, if women could not share the beastliness of the fighting – though many were in some sort of uniform by 1918, relatively few got near the front – they intimately shared its results: the wiping out of lovers, husbands, fathers, brothers and friends. The bereavements that touched enormous numbers of English women during those years have become a historical cliché. We have the stereotype of the bride who never was, who went on to make the emancipated career-woman of the twenties and thirties. Yet do we forget, in that well-known piece of social history, the individual roots of it? How fresh that tragedy becomes in these pages.

But first and foremost the poems mourn for the dead.

The note of grief is twofold: personal and general. Some poems simply relate the death of (or the anxiety for) the one loved. There is the delicate beauty of Katherine Tynan's 'A Girl's Song'; there is the bare account given in Eleanor Farjeon's 'Easter Monday'; or there is the wider perspective, yet still intensely personal nature, of 'Afterwards', Margaret Postgate Cole's bitter elegy (one of the best poems, as she is one of the best poets):

And if these years have made you into a pit-prop,
To carry the twisting galleries of the world's reconstruction
(Where you may thank God, I suppose
That they set you the sole stay of a nasty corner)
What use is it to you? What use
To have your body lying here
In Sheer, underneath the larches?

Each of these various poems share the same stark cry: you were here, now you are dead. Meanwhile Charlotte Mew's poems, with their long marvellous alliterations, are imbued with suffering sympathy for bereaved women.

To those who sit today with their great Dead, hands in their hands,
eyes in their eyes,
At one with Love, at one with Grief: blind to the scattered things and
changing skies.

Some poems turn to the relative stranger, the Unknown Soldier. Here is the second kind of mourning: grief for the millions dead. Sometimes the elegy is spoken directly for all, as in Margaret

Postgate Cole's fine 'The Falling Leaves', a lament for the wholesale sacrifice of youth.

The centre is elegiac; but much else clusters around it. Authentic writing comes out of recording the home scene – the main option open to women writers. At home there is physical safety: despite Nancy Cunard's deadly serious description of 'Zeppelins', there is no continuous Blitz to endure. Yet the grind, along with the joking, is there: working-class poverty, middle-class war-shortages, officers' last leaves, wistful rural backwaters seen at all income-levels and tenderly described in the Georgian tradition; Jingoism rampant; London both grim and feckless; hospitals; soldiers wounded and unwounded; public schools; anxious mothers contemplating their small sons; varieties of war work, including the ubiquitous socks – all done from a middle-class viewpoint, despite the sallies into Kiplingesque Cockney.

Others get over something of the physical chaos of war itself. You sense it in May Sinclair's description of an army in retreat. Her testimony and that of other nurses or V.A.D.s is fascinating since they knew, if not the fighting, at least its immediate results – the extraordinary streams of casualties. At their best they supplement the descriptions of trench warfare by the male poets. Such 'service' poems feel active – part of the action. Some positively burst with praise for the 'grit' and 'pluck' of the men, marching or wounded or dying.

To plunge into the eye of war's hurricane – the fighting itself – required the use of strong imaginative devices. Some work, others not. The transferred voice is especially risky. To go 'Over the Top' as a Cockney private who reverts to God at the last with never a hint of an eff or a blind – this produces touching rather than good poetry. It is simply a measure of the yearning 'to be there', half romantic, half altruistic, an odd mixture – giving grounds for the use of that famous smear-word 'sentimental', which has been so generously applied down the critical ages to all parts of women's poetry.

Sentimentality and patriotism certainly went together during the Great War years. Nowadays, we have less time for Rupert Brooke and his solemn young heroism. We listen now to Sassoon and Owen – reluctant heroes both, though in the end they both stayed submissive to the high-minded macho ethic of the English officer. In the same way, some of the poetry here (and not only the Jingo jingles, but also some much finer) must read dated simply because it embraces confidently the patriotic, and religious, English cause.

Even Alice Meynell's 'Summer in England, 1914', which with handsome outrage draws the contrast between the beauty of the English countryside and the horror of the slaughter, submits to this twin ethic by the poem's end. She tells herself:

> Chide thou no more, O thou unsacrificed!
> The soldier dying dies upon a kiss,
> The very kiss of Christ.

The reluctant implication is: That very horror is necessary to protect that very beauty, that peace.

Unreservedly May Wedderburn Cannan in 'Rouen', with Masefield-like memory, expresses the patriotic excitement:

> Can you recall the parcels that we made them for the railroad,
> Crammed and bulging parcels held together by their string,
> And the voices of the sergeants who called the Drafts together,
> And the agony and splendour when they stood to save the King?

This is the poetry of England, inalienable from Honour, Duty, God, Christ and Sacrifice. This poetry sees as glorious not war itself but certainly the sacrifice of youth. And it accepts that purposeful Sacrifice with enormous gratitude. All flows from Duty. That duty is the world task of keeping alive English values; and then of guarding the sanctity of the English hearth and homeland against the militaristic enemy that threatens all this. If we don't remember the archaic glow of belief in the Imperial task, we lose the idealistic moving force behind 'Lamplight', also by May Wedderburn Cannan. If we don't remember that in 1914 middle-class England was a Christian country, we lose the numinous glow behind the word 'England'. In short, the orthodox Great War belief in the English cause against the Germans, and in the backing of an English God – and great gratitude to the protagonists of all this, the English fighting men – is of the essence in many of these poems. Helen Hamilton herself, that diagnostician of hypocrisy, spells out the received wisdom that the men are dying for the women. Thus – so the received wisdom goes on – the women themselves, the embodiment of Mother England at her most precious, shall live on to ensure the race in freedom and in peace.

The religious metaphor often takes over for the patriotic: the fighting men become Christ on Calvary (sacrificing themselves, and being sacrificed, for Love and Peace). Lucy Whitmell's 'Christ in Flanders' is full, over-full, of this idea. It vies with Madeline Ida Bedford's 'The Parson's Job' as the most sermonising poem in the book. (Both are of course preaching acceptance of the war to the working classes.) But Margaret Sackville's 'Sacrament' is quite a fine sensuous mystic example of the genre (widespread in those years).

Sometimes the poet, as Mary H. J. Henderson in 'An Incident', goes as far as identifying herself with Mary, Christ's mother, sharing humbly in the Sacrifice. Not too far into the book is Helen Hamilton's 'The Romancing Poet'. The two may be enjoyed together – one of the pleasurable pairings Catherine Reilly's wide net offers to the historian.

Christ, then, is crucified, and the duty of the woman, bereaved and despairing, becomes clear. She will live her life as the dead one bequeathed it to her. She will immortalise him in her obedience to the values for which he died. To question those values is to question the Sacrifice itself – impossible. For then his death must become not only horrible but also meaningless.

Therefore, as the death toll mounts, and bitterness grows in place of enthusiasm, it grows only against the enemy. This is the mood of Elinor Jenkins' 'Dulce Et Decorum?'. It is the personal mood of revenge which acquiesced in the grand 'slogging match' between the Powers of the later war years.

It is possibly easier to know that you yourself will probably be dying at random for nothing very much that you can see than to agree that your loved one has done so, with all the disloyalty that that implies. These were the respective hard truths that faced, and divided, men and women during the Great War. The stiff-upper-lip tradition cannot have helped – both sexes feeling they had to cheer each other on. 'We dare not weep who must be brave in battle,' writes Iris Tree. Did this sort of well-meant stoicism among women come over as callous to the men – the background perhaps to the hurt of Sassoon's lines?

And so I read many of the 'patriotic' poems with mixed emotion. They read to me not of superficiality or of hypocrisy, but more of a fearsome desperate nobility. It is the nobility of people who felt sucked into an inevitable tide. In this fated atmosphere even those who came to distrust the cause could be seduced by the excitement of war, as Vera Brittain brilliantly shows in her *Testament of Youth*.

And 'Love' – how often the word becomes a double shorthand for love of country and for personal love, both divinely elevated. The belief, the hope, may be simple: that Love must conquer Death in the end. Iris Tree's impressive 'Of all who died in silence far away' ends on this thought. Yet here is a poem which shifts away from comfortable patriotism. She evokes the soldier rather more as a tortured, deserted Christ.

Less abstractly, others trust in love, feeling more personally that the loved one cannot die, that he lives on within the woman's heart, and that a personal bargain of remembrance will keep him always somehow alive; or that in the end, somehow, living or dying, all are one. Such a stratagem of hope may come from one who believed in the rightfulness of the Sacrifice, or on the contrary from those who thought it doubtful: it's a way of surviving survival that crosses formal belief. And here I come properly to the other response to the war: protest.

And here also I must raise with bewilderment the near-as-maybe non-presence of women in modern Great War anthologies. For Catherine Reilly has retrieved intelligent and vigorous poetry and verse of scorn and denunciation, well in line with modern dislike of Great War heroics. These poems, whether light or grimly satirical, are the mirror images of some of those mentioned above. Lesbia Thanet's small personal statement makes a starting-place. Elizabeth Chandler Forman's deceptively gentle ballad sends up war nationalism absolutely.

God is dead, say others, war is not only horrible but perhaps futile; certainly run on hypocrisy. The young soldiers are the brave, pathetic dupes of war glory: the war glory that Ruth Comfort Mitchell attacks so resoundingly and rollickingly:

They are braggart attitudes we've worn so long;
They are tinsel platitudes we've sworn so long –

Emily Orr's recruit from the slums is the bottom of the heap, and cannon-fodder for Mother England. And in May Herschel-Clarke's ' "For Valour" ' the working-class woman is the bottom of the civilian heap. (But she's a pleasant get-back to Madeline Ida Bedford's persuasive parson.) Civilians, men and women too, are 'Ghouls' or white-feather bullies (Helen Hamilton); or carrion-flies, in Edith Sitwell's powerful image of war fatigue and war hysteria.

We are the dull blind carrion-fly
That dance and batten. Though God die
Mad from the horror of the light –
The light is mad, too, flecked with blood, –
We dance, we dance, each night.

Peace itself becomes a doubtful quantity. And for some – in Elizabeth Daryush's grand 'For a Survivor of the Mesopotamian Campaign' – it will never be possible again. As for the demobilised, says Vera Brittain with drawled irony, they are for the scrapheap. Going back to the war, Winifred M. Letts describes that lowest of the low, 'The Deserter'. Margery Lawrence, in 'Transport of Wounded in Mesopotamia, 1917', roundly identifies with the soldiers against the civilians in an angrily effective cross-over very different from her simple patriotic lament of a year before.

Given this angry identification with the victim soldiers there is little straight evidence for that feminist protest that repudiates war as the outcome of compulsive male aggressiveness or, anyway, of the patriarchal mode. In fact Catherine Reilly points out how some feminism runs the other way – a wish to be with the men.

Still, S. Gertrude Ford assumes that women left to themselves would not have chosen the war. Interestingly, the one piece ('Women at Munition Making' by Mary Gabrielle Collins) that defines war as a male abomination proceeds from the heart of angel-on-the-hearth anti-feminism. As for the historic emancipation of millions of women out of domestic service into munitions and other factory work, it is the jingoistic Jessie Pope who approves – as long as they quit when the men get home.

But 'Ghouls', with its young men supported against the old, does have an anti-patriarchal ring about it. Meanwhile Gabrielle Elliot's 'Pierrot Goes to War' gently chides macho war romance from deserted Pierrette's point of view. Pauline Barrington may be the first poet in the language to plead against war toys for boys. Mary Webb's bejewelled Tennysonian lament has soldiers playing at the war game generation by generation.

> 'O children, come in from your soldier-play
> In the black bean tents! The night is falling. . . .'

But anti-macho criticism is inherent in many of the anti-war pieces mentioned above.

Protest, and naïve patriotism, and many thoughtful stirrings in between. Yet unity exists, despite the divisions in this 'women's voice'. It exists not only in the grief, but also in the admiration for the man. If one or two doubt his better sense, all agree on his courage. Though the word 'sacrifice' takes on wry overtones in some mouths, all agree that one way or another a sacrifice has been made, glorious, terrible or monstrous, and that it must not be forgotten, nor the men themselves. Ursula Roberts' contempt for the Remembrance ceremony in 'The Cenotaph' is diametrically opposed to Charlotte Mew's 'The Cenotaph 1919'. Yet both are talking about remembrance. Ironically, and from different points of view, this old theme, 'lest we forget', unites all.

I hope that this anthology, like Vera Brittain's autobiography reissued, will make flesh some of the griefs, certainties, doubts and despairs of the English women who lived through the Great War, and that it will redeem them from the clutches of the 'white feather' image. And I wonder, after all, if the invisibility to date of women's poetry on the Great War doesn't stem from something quite deep in the patriarchal mind – the folk memory that nurses that 'white feather' image along – the same which generates a general lack of interest in women's wartime experience, including the endlessly repeated tragic one of bereavement.

The particular furious magnificence of the soldier poets makes it unsurprising that women poets should recede into the background. Yet to be so little known now?

Is there among men, not excluding editors of war-poetry anthologies, the atavistic feeling that war is man's concern, as birth is woman's; and that women quite simply cannot speak on the matter – an illogic which holds sway even when women have done so with knowledge and talent? It would be an understandable illogic. For men in the Great War had to die and women did not; and, moreover, men died in their millions, according to the official and explicit credo, for Mother England – that their women should live, protected, in peace. Deep emotions might well fuel such an illogic, handed down over the decades by patriarchal tradition – that women had nothing to say on the war.

Whether such a deep system has operated, who knows? It is of course nonsense that women have nothing to do with war. Even in the Great War with its huge partitions of the sexes, it was a nonsense: and I do not simply refer to women's war work.

Yet, just as men often feel they have a bit part during childbirth, so women during war-time. I have suggested that many of these poems are about ways to survive survival. They are equally about ways to find a role. Not an easy position, on the 'Rim of the shadow of the Hell'. It led to some loud posturing; it certainly led to many more acts of heart-rending stoical support.

In the end Sassoon's 'Glory of Women' is unfair because it presented women with a catch. If they encouraged their men, they were heartless; but how if (as some courageously did, of course) they had backed out, refused to be brave, opposed the man's own grim determination to act creditably in what was after all a male-run 'show'?

Empathy between the sexes had to operate over the divide of

land and sea, and over a dividing wasteland of experience. Many of these poems reach into that wasteland painfully. Some cross it with triumph.

Judith Kazantzis, London 1981

Chaos of the Night

Unshaken world! Another day of light
After the human chaos of the night . . .

FRANCES CORNFORD

Contents

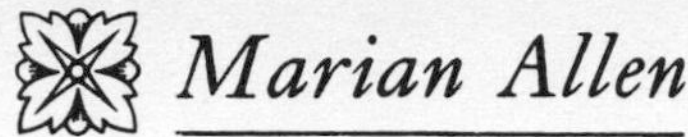

Marian Allen

THE RAIDERS

In shadowy formation up they rise,
Dusky raiders with their bat-like wings.
The night is studded with a thousand eyes
And its dim cloak on desolation flings.
The wind through stay and wire moans and whines,
The engines throb with thrilled expectant breath.
Eighty miles to eastward of the lines
They go and carry with them stings of death.
The spirit of Adventure calls ahead,
They leave the earth behind them battle-bound
And rise untrammelled from the war-stained ground,
Grey moving shadows o'er the lonely dead,
Flying unflinching as an arrow flies
Down the uncharted roadway of the skies.

THE WIND ON THE DOWNS

I like to think of you as brown and tall,
As strong and living as you used to be,
In khaki tunic, Sam Brown belt and all,
And standing there and laughing down at me.
Because they tell me, dear, that you are dead,
Because I can no longer see your face,
You have not died, it is not true, instead
You seek adventure in some other place.
That you are round about me, I believe;
I hear you laughing as you used to do,
Yet loving all the things I think of you;
And knowing you are happy, should I grieve?
You follow and are watchful where I go;
How should you leave me, having loved me so?

We walked along the tow-path, you and I,
Beside the sluggish-moving, still canal;
It seemed impossible that you should die;

Marian Allen

I think of you the same and always shall.
We thought of many things and spoke of few,
And life lay all uncertainly before,
And now I walk alone and think of you,
And wonder what new kingdoms you explore.
Over the railway line, across the grass,
While up above the golden wings are spread,
Flying, ever flying overhead,
Here still I see your khaki figure pass,
And when I leave the meadow, almost wait
That you should open first the wooden gate.

Lilian M. Anderson

LEAVE IN 1917

Moonlight and death were on the Narrow Seas,
moonlight and death and sleep were on the land:
blindfold the lamps of home, but blinding bright
the wheeling, watching, searching lamps of war.
To the lone pilot, homing like a dove,
his England was no England. Thought he not
of night-hushed fields and elms, of sleeping farms
where bats, like swallows, hawked about the eaves,
and the white moonlight still as water lay
upon the farmyard and the shippen roofs.
Thought he of hidden forts and hidden camps,
of furnaces down-slaked to darkness, towns
crouched slumbering beneath the threat of death.
North-west he held till, stooping, he could read
the map-small town of Bedford. Up and on.
Northampton fell behind him. Twenty miles,
and Avon lay, a winding thread of steel,
among its wraith-white meadows.
Low and lower
swept the still wings. Beyond the many roofs,
beyond the chimney-shafts, behind the hills,
the moon hung pallid in an empty sky.
Ached in his throat the scent of morning frost.
The wren-shrill song of every harping wire
was joyful in the silence. Coventry
was yet asleep, but out among the sheds,
new-lit on frosty grass, he found a welcome.

The crystalled dawn grew red, and the sun crept
above the sharp-rimmed hills. And Sheringham,
seeing the rays smoke white athwart the field,
knew that from dawn to dawn, and once again
from dawn to eve, pain-precious every hour,
lay – God be thanked for it! – two days of leave.

. . . He travelled south and west.
And still to him his England was no England;

but, rocking to the motion of the train,
half-sleeping where he stood, and sleeping quite
whenever chance and crowds and courtesy
would give him leave to rest, he dreamt of war,
of flights and stunts and crashes; tattered dreams
of month-old happenings.
Until at last
his drowsiness was stirred by Devon names –
Exeter, Axminster,
Starcross and Dawlish Warren –
and from his dreams he woke to level waves
that broke on tide-wet shallows.
Here was his England, stripped of mail and weapons,
child-sweet and maiden-gentle. Here was Spring,
her feet frost-bright among the daffodils.
Four months ago
when ice hung from the ferns beside the spring
and robins came for crumbs, had Sheringham,
new-wedded, brought his wife to Devonshire.
The little house stood half-way up the hill,
with milk-white walls, and slated paths that went
like stepping-stones, from April to October,
among a foam of flowers. Apple-trees
leaned from the orchard-slopes; the hillside grass
showed apple-green beneath. Four months ago
had ice hung from the ferns beside the spring:
now, as he climbed the hillside, Sheringham
saw snowdrops in the grass, and heard the lambs
in the Prior's Acre and the valley fields
calling and calling. Clear dripped the spring
beside the orchard-gate.
And 'God!' he prayed,
for sunset lay along the upper boughs
of every twisted tree, and emerald dusk
lay stirlessly beneath. And, still as dusk
because she feared to meet her happiness,
his wife stood waiting on the orchard-steeps.

Love came to them, poor Love, with pinions torn –
poor Love, young Love, that should bc auriole-winged.
Scarcely they dared to hold each other close,
young husband and young wife, scarcely to kiss,
lest they should shatter, by their very love,
this rainbow-fragile joy. For every kiss,
however sweet with joy, held lees of tears.
Like bees that garner sunshine-golden honey
against the barren winter, Sheringham
garnered his memories against the morrow.
Here was the slated threshold of his home,
and here his lighted hearth; here daffodils
shone amber in the firelight; here the breath
of violets and rosy hyacinths
clung heavy to the blue and bitter incense
of lately-kindled logs. And sweet, sweet, sweet
the finches singing in the orchard dusk!

Pauline Barrington

'EDUCATION'

The rain is slipping, dripping down the street;
The day is grey as ashes on the hearth.
The children play with soldiers made of tin,
        While you sew
        Row after row.

The tears are slipping, dripping one by one;
Your son has shot and wounded his small brother.
The mimic battle's ended with a sob,
        While you dream
        Over your seam.

The blood is slipping, dripping drop by drop;
The men are dying in the trenches' mud.
The bullets search the quick among the dead.
        While you drift,
        The Gods sift.

The ink is slipping, dripping from the pens,
On papers, White and Orange, Red and Grey, –
History for the children of tomorrow, –
        While you prate
        About Fate.

War is slipping, dripping death on earth.
If the child is father of the man,
Is the toy gun father of the Krupps?
        For Christ's sake think!
        While you sew
        Row after row.

Madeline Ida Bedford

MUNITION WAGES

Earning high wages? Yus,
   Five quid a week.
A woman, too, mind you,
   I calls it dim sweet.

Ye'are asking some questions –
   But bless yer, here goes:
I spends the whole racket
   On good times and clothes.

Me saving? Elijah!
   Yer do think I'm mad.
I'm acting the lady,
   But – I ain't living bad.

I'm having life's good times.
   See 'ere, it's like this:
The 'oof come o' danger,
   A touch-and-go bizz.

We're all here today, mate,
   Tomorrow – perhaps dead,
If Fate tumbles on us
   And blows up our shed.

Afraid! Are yer kidding?
   With money to spend!
Years back I wore tatters,
   Now – silk stockings, mi friend!

I've bracelets and jewellery,
   Rings envied by friends;
A sergeant to swank with,
   And something to lend.

I drive out in taxis,
   Do theatres in style.
And this is mi verdict –
   It is jolly worth while.

Worth while, for tomorrow
  If I'm blown to the sky,
I'll have repaid mi wages
  In death – and pass by.

THE PARSON'S JOB

What do you want
Coming to this 'ere 'ell?
Ain't it enough to know he's dead,
Killed by a bit o' German lead?
What! – the Lord means well?

I guess ye' are daft!
He's one o' the good'uns, Jim;
Nature's gentleman, rough but true.
He didn't know 'ow to sin,
But – what is that to you?

You make me sick.
Why should he die,
When forger Wright wins a V.C.
And criminal Kelly catches a spy?
That don't spell Justice to me.

Get out, or I'll strike you down.
I'm carrying his kid.
Do you call that fair?
Gawd – no wonder I wants to gib;
Our first-born, and his father – where?

You hold yer tongue.
What he said of our child
Ain't for you to be teaching me.
He called it 'Our little blossom wild'.
Why – can't yer let me be!

I hate your religion;
I don't want gold;
I only want my man.
What? It's in me to enfold
Jim in my babyland?

Gawd bless yer, Parson,
I'll try to think right
Upon my widowed way.
So Jim ain't quite out o' sight?
Teach me – ow – to pray.

Maud Anna Bell

FROM A TRENCH

Out here the dogs of war run loose,
   Their whipper-in is Death;
Across the spoilt and battered fields
   We hear their sobbing breath.
The fields where grew the living corn
   Are heavy with our dead;
Yet still the fields at home are green
   And I have heard it said:

That –
There are crocuses at Nottingham!
Wild crocuses at Nottingham!
Blue crocuses at Nottingham!
Though here the grass is red.

There are little girls at Nottingham
   Who do not dread the Boche,
Young girls at school at Nottingham
   (Lord! how I need a wash!).
There are little boys at Nottingham
   Who never heard a gun;
There are silly fools at Nottingham
   Who think we're here for fun.

When –
There are crocuses at Nottingham!
Young crocus buds at Nottingham!
Thousands of buds at Nottingham
Ungathered by the Hun.

But here we trample down the grass
   Into a purple slime;
There lives no tree to give the birds
   House room in pairing-time.
We live in holes, like cellar rats,
   But through the noise and smell

Maud Anna Bell

I often see those crocuses
  Of which the people tell.

Why!
There are crocuses at Nottingham!
Bright crocuses at Nottingham!
Real crocuses at Nottingham!
Because we're here in Hell.

Nora Bomford

DRAFTS

Waking to darkness; early silence broken
By seagulls' cries, and something undefined
And far away. Through senses half-awoken,
A vague enquiry drifts into one's mind.
What's happening? Down the hill a movement quickens
And leaps to recognition round the turning –
Then one's heart wakes, and grasps the fact, and sickens –
'Are we down-hearted' . . . 'Keep the homefires burning'.
They go to God-knows-where, with songs of Blighty,
While I'm in bed, and ribbons in my nightie.

Sex, nothing more, constituent no greater
Than those which make an eyebrow's slant or fall,
In origin, sheer accident, which, later,
Decides the biggest differences of all.
And, through a war, involves the chance of death
Against a life of physical normality –
So dreadfully safe! O, damn the shibboleth
Of sex! God knows we've equal personality.
Why should men face the dark while women stay
To live and laugh and meet the sun each day.

They've gone. The drumming escort throbs the distance,
And down the hill the seagulls' cries are rife
And clamorous. But in their shrill persistence
I think they're telling me – 'We're all one Life'.
As much one life as when we flamed together,
As linked, as indivisible, as then;
When nothing's separate, does it matter whether
We live as women or we die as men?
Or swoop as seagulls! Everything is part
Of one supreme intent, the deathless heart.

Sybil Bristowe

OVER THE TOP

Ten more minutes! – Say yer prayers,
Read yer Bibles, pass the rum!
Ten more minutes! Strike me dumb,
'Ow they creeps on unawares,
Those blooming minutes. Nine. It's queer,
I'm sorter stunned. It ain't with fear!

Eight. It's like as if a frog
Waddled round in your inside,
Cold as ice-blocks, straddle wide,
Tired o' waiting. Where's the grog?
Seven. I'll play yer pitch and toss –
Six. – I wins, and tails yer loss.

'Nother minute sprinted by
'Fore I knowed it; only Four
(Break 'em into seconds) more
'Twixt us and Eternity.
Every word I've ever said
Seems a-shouting in my head.

Three. Larst night a little star
Fairly shook up in the sky,
Didn't like the lullaby
Rattled by the dogs of War.
Funny thing – that star all white
Saw old Blighty, too, larst night.

Two. I ain't ashamed o' prayers,
They're only wishes sent ter God
Bits o' plants from bloody sod
Trailing up His golden stairs.
Ninety seconds – Well, who cares!
One –
No fife, no blare, no drum –
Over the Top – to Kingdom Come!

Vera Brittain

THE LAMENT OF THE DEMOBILISED

'Four years,' some say consolingly. 'Oh well,
What's that? You're young. And then it must have been
A very fine experience for you!'
And they forget
How others stayed behind and just got on –
Got on the better since we were away.
And we came home and found
They had achieved, and men revered their names,
But never mentioned ours;
And no one talked heroics now, and we
Must just go back and start again once more.
'You threw four years into the melting-pot –
Did you indeed!' these others cry. 'Oh well,
The more fool you!'
And we're beginning to agree with them.

PERHAPS—

(To R.A.L. Died of Wounds in France, December 23rd, 1915)

Perhaps some day the sun will shine again,
  And I shall see that still the skies are blue,
And feel once more I do not live in vain,
  Although bereft of You.

Perhaps the golden meadows at my feet
  Will make the sunny hours of Spring seem gay,
And I shall find the white May blossoms sweet,
  Though You have passed away.

Perhaps the summer woods will shimmer bright,
  And crimson roses once again be fair,
And autumn harvest fields a rich delight,
  Although You are not there.

Perhaps some day I shall not shrink in pain
  To see the passing of the dying year,

And listen to the Christmas songs again,
  Although You cannot hear.

But, though kind Time may many joys renew,
  There is one greatest joy I shall not know
Again, because my heart for loss of You
  Was broken, long ago.

1st London General Hospital
February 1916

TO MY BROTHER*

(In Memory of July 1st, 1916)

Your battle-wounds are scars upon my heart,
  Received when in that grand and tragic 'show'
You played your part
  Two years ago,

And silver in the summer morning sun
  I see the symbol of your courage glow –
That Cross you won
  Two years ago.

Though now again you watch the shrapnel fly,
  And hear the guns that daily louder grow,
As in July
  Two years ago,

May you endure to lead the Last Advance
  And with your men pursue the flying foe
As once in France
  Two years ago.

* Captain E. H. Brittain, M.C. Written four days before his death in action in the Austrian offensive on the Italian Front, June 15th, 1918.

May Wedderburn Cannan

LAMPLIGHT

We planned to shake the world together, you and I
Being young, and very wise;
Now in the light of the green shaded lamp
Almost I see your eyes
Light with the old gay laughter; you and I
Dreamed greatly of an Empire in those days,
Setting our feet upon laborious ways,
And all you asked of fame
Was crossed swords in the Army List,
My Dear, against your name.

We planned a great Empire together, you and I,
Bound only by the sea;
Now in the quiet of a chill Winter's night
Your voice comes hushed to me
Full of forgotten memories: you and I
Dreamed great dreams of our future in those days,
Setting our feet on undiscovered ways,
And all I asked of fame
A scarlet cross on my breast, my Dear,
For the swords by your name.

We shall never shake the world together, you and I,
For you gave your life away;
And I think my heart was broken by the war,
Since on a summer day
You took the road we never spoke of: you and I
Dreamed greatly of an Empire in those days;
You set your feet upon the Western ways
And have no need of fame –
There's a scarlet cross on my breast, my Dear,
And a torn cross with your name.

December 1916

May Wedderburn Cannan

ROUEN

26 April–25 May 1915

Early morning over Rouen, hopeful, high, courageous morning,
And the laughter of adventure and the steepness of the stair,
And the dawn across the river, and the wind across the bridges,
And the empty littered station and the tired people there.

Can you recall those mornings and the hurry of awakening,
And the long-forgotten wonder if we should miss the way,
And the unfamiliar faces, and the coming of provisions,
And the freshness and the glory of the labour of the day?

Hot noontide over Rouen, and the sun upon the city,
Sun and dust unceasing, and the glare of cloudless skies,
And the voices of the Indians and the endless stream of soldiers,
And the clicking of the tatties, and the buzzing of the flies.

Can you recall those noontides and the reek of steam and coffee,
Heavy-laden noontides with the evening's peace to win,
And the little piles of Woodbines, and the sticky soda bottles,
And the crushes in the 'Parlour', and the letters coming in?

Quiet night-time over Rouen, and the station full of soldiers,
All the youth and pride of England from the ends of all the earth;
And the rifles piled together, and the creaking of the sword-belts,
And the faces bent above them, and the gay, heart-breaking
mirth.

Can I forget the passage from the cool white-bedded Aid Post
Past the long sun-blistered coaches of the khaki Red Cross train
To the truck train full of wounded, and the weariness and
laughter,
And 'Good-bye, and thank you, Sister', and the empty yards
again?

Can you recall the parcels that we made them for the railroad,
Crammed and bulging parcels held together by their string,
And the voices of the sergeants who called the Drafts together,
And the agony and splendour when they stood to save the King?

May Wedderburn Cannan

Can you forget their passing, the cheering and the waving,
The little group of people at the doorway of the shed,
The sudden awful silence when the last train swung to darkness,
And the lonely desolation, and the mocking stars o'erhead?

Can you recall the midnights, and the footsteps of night
watchers,
Men who came from darkness and went back to dark again,
And the shadows on the rail-lines and the all-inglorious labour,
And the promise of the daylight firing blue the window-pane?

Can you recall the passing through the kitchen door to morning,
Morning very still and solemn breaking slowly on the town,
And the early coastways engines that had met the ships at
daybreak,
And the Drafts just out from England, and the day shift coming
down?

Can you forget returning slowly, stumbling on the cobbles,
And the white-decked Red Cross barges dropping seawards for
the tide,
And the search for English papers, and the blessed cool of water,
And the peace of half-closed shutters that shut out the world
outside?

Can I forget the evenings and the sunsets on the island,
And the tall black ships at anchor far below our balcony,
And the distant call of bugles, and the white wine in the glasses,
And the long line of the street lamps, stretching Eastwards to the
sea?

. . . When the world slips slow to darkness, when the office fire
burns lower,
My heart goes out to Rouen, Rouen all the world away;
When other men remember I remember our Adventure
And the trains that go from Rouen at the ending of the day.

'SINCE THEY HAVE DIED'

Since they have died to give us gentleness,
And hearts kind with contentment and quiet mirth,
Let us who live give also happiness
And love, that's born of pity, to the earth.

For, I have thought, some day they may lie sleeping
Fogetting all the weariness and pain,
And smile to think their world is in our keeping,
And laughter come back to the earth again.

February 1916

LOVE, 1916

One said to me, 'Seek Love, for he is Joy
Called by another name'.
A Second said, 'Seek Love, for he is Power
Which is called Fame'.
Last said a Third, 'Seek Love, his name is Peace'.
I called him thrice,
And answer came, 'Love now
Is christened Sacrifice'.

August 1916

Isabel C. Clarke

ANNIVERSARY OF THE GREAT RETREAT

(1915)

Now a whole year has waxed and waned and whitened
  Over the mounds that marked that grim advance;
The winter snows have lain, the spring flowers brightened,
  On those belovèd graves of Northern France.

Caudry, Le Cateau, Landrécies, are written
  In our sad hearts with letters as of flame,
Where our young dead still lie, untimely smitten,
  In graves still unredeemed that bear no name.

And those who saw them spoke of the 'boy-faces'
  The English soldiers wore; they heard them sing
As they went forth to their appointed places,
  Who when night fell lay unremembering. . . .

O England, sing their fame in song and story,
  Who knew Death's victory not Life's defeat;
Be their names written on thy roll of glory,
  Who fought and perished in the Great Retreat!

These held thy high tradition in their keeping
  This flower of all a nation's youth and pride
And safe they hold it still in their last sleeping;
  They heard thy call and answered it and died. . . .

And by those graves that mark their proud surrender
  In days to come each one that lingereth
Shall sadly think of all their vanished splendour,
  'Contemptible', but faithful unto death.

So we press forward, step by step redeeming
  Each hallowed spot our dead have sanctified,
That we may whisper to them in their dreaming,
  The Victory is ours because you died. . . .

Margaret Postgate Cole

THE FALLING LEAVES

November 1915

Today, as I rode by,
I saw the brown leaves dropping from their tree
In a still afternoon,
When no wind whirled them whistling to the sky,
But thickly, silently,
They fell, like snowflakes wiping out the noon;
And wandered slowly thence
For thinking of a gallant multitude
Which now all withering lay,
Slain by no wind of age or pestilence,
But in their beauty strewed
Like snowflakes falling on the Flemish clay.

AFTERWARDS

Oh, my beloved, shall you and I
Ever be young again, be young again?
The people that were resigned said to me
– Peace will come and you will lie
Under the larches up in Sheer,
Sleeping,
And eating strawberries and cream and cakes –
        O cakes, O cakes, O cakes, from Fuller's!
And quite forgetting there's a train to town,
Plotting in an afternoon the new curves for the world.

And peace came. And lying in Sheer
I look round at the corpses of the larches
Whom they slew to make pit-props
For mining the coal for the great armies.
And think, a pit-prop cannot move in the wind,
Nor have red manes hanging in spring from its branches,
And sap making the warm air sweet.
Though you planted it out on the hill again it would be dead.

And if these years have made you into a pit-prop,
To carry the twisting galleries of the world's reconstruction
(Where you may thank God, I suppose
That they set you the sole stay of a nasty corner)
What use is it to you? What use
To have your body lying here
In Sheer, underneath the larches?

PRAEMATURI

When men are old, and their friends die,
They are not so sad,
Because their love is running slow,
And cannot spring from the wound with so sharp a pain;
And they are happy with many memories,
And only a little while to be alone.

But we are young, and our friends are dead
Suddenly, and our quick love is torn in two;
So our memories are only hopes that came to nothing.
We are left alone like old men; we should be dead
– But there are years and years in which we shall still be young.

THE VETERAN

May, 1916

We came upon him sitting in the sun,
  Blinded by war, and left. And past the fence
There came young soldiers from the Hand and Flower,
  Asking advice of his experience.

And he said this, and that, and told them tales,
  And all the nightmares of each empty head
Blew into air; then, hearing us beside,
  'Poor chaps, how'd they know what it's like?' he said.

And we stood there, and watched him as he sat,
  Turning his sockets where they went away,
Until it came to one of us to ask
  'And you're – how old?'
        'Nineteen, the third of May.'

Mary Gabrielle Collins

WOMEN AT MUNITION MAKING

Their hands should minister unto the flame of life,
Their fingers guide
The rosy teat, swelling with milk,
To the eager mouth of the suckling babe
Or smooth with tenderness,
Softly and soothingly,
The heated brow of the ailing child.
Or stray among the curls
Of the boy or girl, thrilling to mother love.
But now,
Their hands, their fingers
Are coarsened in munition factories.
Their thoughts, which should fly
Like bees among the sweetest mind flowers,
Gaining nourishment for the thoughts to be,
Are bruised against the law,
'Kill, kill'.
They must take part in defacing and destroying the natural body
Which, certainly during this dispensation
Is the shrine of the spirit.
O God!
Throughout the ages we have seen,
Again and again
Men by Thee created
Cancelling each other.
And we have marvelled at the seeming annihilation
Of Thy work.
But this goes further,
Taints the fountain head,
Mounts like a poison to the Creator's very heart.
O God!
Must It anew be sacrificed on earth?

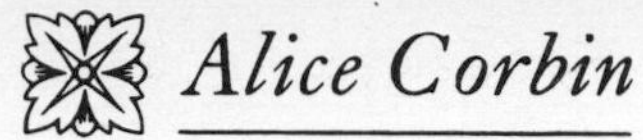

FALLEN

He was wounded and he fell in the midst of hoarse shouting.
The tide passed, and the waves came and whispered about his
ankles.
Far off he heard a cock crow – children laughing,
Rising at dawn to greet the storm of petals
Shaken from apple-boughs; he heard them cry,
And turned again to find the breast of her,
And sank confusèd with a little sigh . . .
Thereafter water running, and a voice
That seemed to stir and flutter through the trenches
And set dead lips to talking . . .

Wreckage was mingled with the storm of petals . . .

He felt her near him, and the weight dropped off –
Suddenly . . .

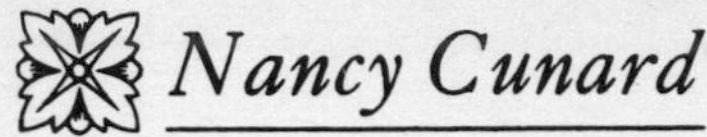

ZEPPELINS

I saw the people climbing up the street
Maddened with war and strength and thought to kill;
And after followed Death, who held with skill
His torn rags royally, and stamped his feet.

The fires flamed up and burnt the serried town,
Most where the sadder, poorer houses were;
Death followed with proud feet and smiling stare,
And the mad crowds ran madly up and down.

And many died and hid in unfound places
In the black ruins of the frenzied night;
And Death still followed in his surplice, white
And streaked in imitation of their faces.

. . .

But in the morning men began again
To mock Death following in bitter pain.

Elizabeth Daryush

FLANDERS FIELDS

Here the scanted daisy glows
Glorious as the carmined rose;
Here the hill-top's verdure mean
Fair is with unfading green;
Here, where sorrow still must tread,
All her graves are garlanded.

And still, O glad passer-by
Of the fields of agony,
Lower laughter's voice, and bare
Thy head in the valley where
Poppies bright and rustling wheat
Are a desert to love's feet.

FOR A SURVIVOR OF THE MESOPOTAMIAN CAMPAIGN

War's wasted era is a desert shore,
As know those who have passèd there, a place
Where, within sound of swoll'n destruction's roar,
Wheel the wild vultures, lust and terror base;
Where, making ready for them, stalk the grim
Barbarian forms, hunger, disease and pain,
Who, slashing all life's beauty limb from limb,
Crush it as folly on their stony plain.

A desert: – those too who, as thou, have been
Followers of war's angel, Sacrifice,
(Stern striders to beyond brute torment's scene,
Soarers above the swerves of fear and vice)
Know that the lightning of his ghostly gaze
Has wrecked for them for ever earth's small ways.

Elizabeth Daryush

SUBALTERNS

She said to one: 'How glows
My heart at the hot thought
Of battle's glorious throes!'
He said: 'For us who fought
Are icy memories
That must for ever freeze
The sunny hours they bought.'

She said to one: 'How light
Must be your freed heart now,
After the heavy fight!'
He said: 'Well, I don't know . . .
The war gave one a shake,
Somehow, knocked one awake . . .
Now, life's so deadly slow.'

UNKNOWN WARRIOR

Not that broad path chose he, which whoso wills
May tread, if he but pay the fatal price,
And for such sweets as earthly life extils,
Slaughter his heaven-born soul in sacrifice.

But he, though loving these, cast yet with strong
Hand all aside, and took the obscure way,
Which few may find, or, finding, follow long, –
O let not weak regrets hinder me, nay,

Health, wealth, fame, friendship, all that I hold dear,
I'll spend, nor seek return. O what dark crown
Be his, he cares not, who thus gives; how near
May hang yet his lost laurels of renown:

Yea, who dares thus die, haply he may see,
Suddenly, unsought immortality.

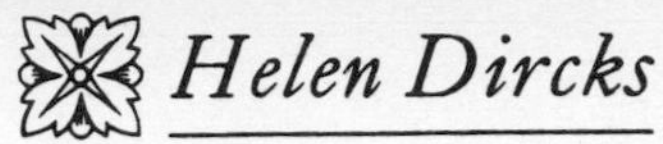

Helen Dircks

AFTER BOURLON WOOD

In one of London's most exclusive haunts,
Amid the shining lights and table ware,
We sat, where meagre Mistress Ration flaunts
Herself in syncopated music there.

He was a Major twenty-six years old,
Back from the latest party of the Hun,
He said: 'The beastly blighters had me bowled
Almost before the picnic had begun.

'By Jove! I was particularly cross,
I had looked forward to a little fling!
(These censored wine lists have me at a loss.)
But what have you been doing, dear old thing?'

'I go to bed,' I said, 'at half-past ten,
And lead the life of any simple Waac –
Alas! a meatless, sweetless one – and then
I have a little joy when you come back.

'But mostly life is dull upon this isle,
And is inclined to be a trifle limp.'
'I hate,' he said, 'the Hun to cramp my style,
We'll try and give it just a little crimp.'

'On Saturday,' I cried, 'we stop at one:
To help you with the crimping would be grand!'
'Sorry,' he said, 'it simply can't be done,
I've got a most unpleasant job on hand.'

'Unpleasant job!' I asked. 'What do you mean?'
'I would,' he said, 'avoid it if I could,
But Georgius Rex, it seems, is awfully keen
To give me the M.C. for being good.'

Helen Dircks

LONDON IN WAR

White faces,
Like helpless petals on the stream,
Swirl by,
Or linger
And then go. . . .

Ancient summer burns
Where green trees branch
From palaces of stone;
I see the brightness
Through a throbbing gloom,
While death rattles
To a tripping melody. . . .

Hot laughter comes,
With tears of ice,
Where War is God
And God is War;
For He has torn
The gallant spirits that He gave,
Till joy is agony,
And agony is joy. . . .

Night falls with its olden touch,
But sleep comes
Like a bloody man,
And the stars
Are wounded birds
That fall
For ever. . . .

Eva Dobell

PLUCK

Crippled for life at seventeen,
   His great eyes seem to question why:
With both legs smashed it might have been
   Better in that grim trench to die
   Than drag maimed years out helplessly.

A child – so wasted and so white,
   He told a lie to get his way,
To march, a man with men, and fight
   While other boys are still at play.
   A gallant lie your heart will say.

So broke with pain, he shrinks in dread
   To see the 'dresser' drawing near;
And winds the clothes about his head
   That none may see his heart-sick fear.
   His shaking, strangled sobs you hear.

But when the dreaded moment's there
   He'll face us all, a soldier yet,
Watch his bared wounds with unmoved air,
   (Though tell-tale lashes still are wet),
   And smoke his woodbine cigarette.

GRAMOPHONE TUNES

Through the long ward the gramophone
   Grinds out its nasal melodies:
'Where did you get that girl?' it shrills.
   The patients listen at their ease,
Through clouds of strong tobacco-smoke:
   The gramophone can always please.

The Welsh boy has it by his bed,
   (He's lame – one leg was blown away).
He'll lie propped up with pillows there,

And wind the handle half the day.
His neighbour, with the shattered arm,
Picks out the records he must play.

Jock with his crutches beats the time;
The gunner, with his head close-bound,
Listens with puzzled, patient smile:
(Shell-shock – he cannot hear a sound).
The others join in from their beds,
And send the chorus rolling round.

Somehow for me these common tunes
Can never sound the same again:
They've magic now to thrill my heart
And bring before me, clear and plain,
Man that is master of his flesh,
And has the laugh of death and pain.

NIGHT DUTY

The pain and laughter of the day are done,
So strangely hushed and still the long ward seems,
Only the Sister's candle softly beams.
Clear from the church near by the clock strikes 'one';
And all are wrapt away in secret sleep and dreams.

They bandied talk and jest from bed to bed;
Now sleep has touched them with a subtle change.
They lie here deep withdrawn, remote and strange;
A dimly outlined shape, a tumbled head.
Through what far lands do now their wand'ring spirits range?

Here one cries sudden on a sobbing breath,
Gripped in the clutch of some incarnate fear:
What terror through the darkness draweth near?
What memory of carnage and of death?
What vanished scenes of dread to his closed eyes appear?

And one laughs out with an exultant joy.
An athlete he – Maybe his young limbs strain
In some remembered game, and not in vain
To win his side the goal – Poor crippled boy,
Who in the waking world will never run again.

One murmurs soft and low a woman's name;
And here a vet'ran soldier, calm and still
As sculptured marble sleeps, and roams at will
Through eastern lands where sunbeams scorch like flame,
By rich bazaar and town, and wood-wrapt snow-crowned hill.

Through the wide open window one great star,
Swinging her lamp above the pear-tree high,
Looks in upon these dreaming forms that lie
So near in body, yet in soul as far
As those bright worlds thick strewn on that vast depth of sky.

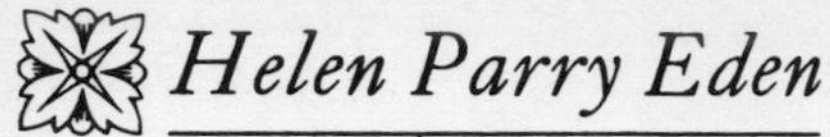

A VOLUNTEER

He had no heart for war, its ways and means,
Its train of machinations and machines,
Its murky provenance, its flagrant ends;
His soul, unpledged for his own dividends,
He had not ventured for a nation's spoils.
So had he sighed for England in her toils
Of greed, was't like his pulse would beat less blithe
To see the Teuton shells on Rotherhithe
And Mayfair – so each body had 'scaped its niche,
The wretched poor, the still more wretched rich?
Why had he sought the struggle and its pain?
Lest little girls with linked hands in the lane
Should look 'You did not shield us!' as they wended
Across his window when the war was ended.

PIERROT GOES TO WAR

In the sheltered garden, pale beneath the moon,
(Drenched with swaying fragrance, redolent with June!)
There, among the shadows, some one lingers yet –
Pierrot, the lover, parts from Pierrette.

Bugles, bugles, bugles, blaring down the wind,
Sound the flaming challenge – *Leave your dreams behind!*
Come away from shadows, turn your back on June –
Pierrot, go forward to face the golden noon!

In the muddy trenches, black and torn and still,
(How the charge swept over, to break against the hill!)
Huddled in the shadows, boyish figures lie –
They whom Death, saluting, called upon to die.

Bugles, ghostly bugles, whispering down the wind –
Dreams too soon are over, gardens left behind.
Only shadows linger, for love does not forget –
Pierrot goes forward – but what of Pierrette?

October, 1917

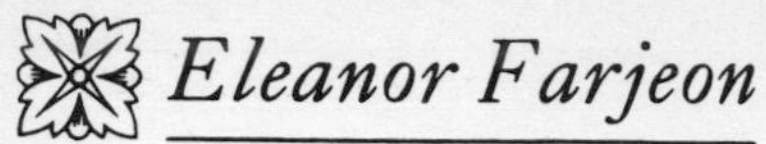

Eleanor Farjeon

EASTER MONDAY

(In Memoriam E.T.)

In the last letter that I had from France
You thanked me for the silver Easter egg
Which I had hidden in the box of apples
You liked to munch beyond all other fruit.
You found the egg the Monday before Easter,
And said, 'I will praise Easter Monday now –
It was such a lovely morning'. Then you spoke
Of the coming battle and said, 'This is the eve.
Good-bye. And may I have a letter soon.'

That Easter Monday was a day for praise,
It was such a lovely morning. In our garden
We sowed our earliest seeds, and in the orchard
The apple-bud was ripe. It was the eve.
There are three letters that you will not get.

April 9th, 1917

PEACE

I

I am as awful as my brother War,
I am the sudden silence after clamour.
I am the face that shows the seamy scar
When blood has lost its frenzy and its glamour.
Men in my pause shall know the cost at last
That is not to be paid in triumphs or tears,
Men will begin to judge the thing that's past
As men will judge it in a hundred years.

Nations! whose ravenous engines must be fed
Endlessly with the father and the son,
My naked light upon your darkness, dread! –
By which ye shall behold what ye have done:

Whereon, more like a vulture than a dove,
Ye set my seal in hatred, not in love.

II

Let no man call me good. I am not blest.
My single virtue is the end of crimes,
I only am the period of unrest,
The ceasing of the horrors of the times;
My good is but the negative of ill,
Such ill as bends the spirit with despair,
Such ill as makes the nations' soul stand still
And freeze to stone beneath its Gorgon glare.

Be blunt, and say that peace is but a state
Wherein the active soul is free to move,
And nations only show as mean or great
According to the spirit then they prove. –
O which of ye whose battle-cry is Hate
Will first in peace dare shout the name of Love?

'NOW THAT YOU TOO'

Now that you too must shortly go the way
Which in these bloodshot years uncounted men
Have gone in vanishing armies day by day,
And in their numbers will not come again:
I must not strain the moments of our meeting
Striving each look, each accent, not to miss,
Or question of our parting and our greeting,
Is this the last of all? is this – or this?

Last sight of all it may be with these eyes,
Last touch, last hearing, since eyes, hands, and ears,
Even serving love, are our mortalities,
And cling to what they own in mortal fears: –
But oh, let end what will, I hold you fast
By immortal love, which has no first or last.

S. Gertrude Ford

'A FIGHT TO A FINISH'

'Fight the year out!' the War-lords said:
What said the dying among the dead?

'To the last man!' cried the profiteers:
What said the poor in the starveling years?

'War is good!' yelled the Jingo-kind:
What said the wounded, the maimed and blind?

'Fight on!' the Armament-kings besought:
Nobody asked what the women thought.

'On!' echoed Hate where the fiends kept tryst:
Asked the Church, even, what said Christ?

NATURE IN WAR-TIME

The banished thrush, the homeless rook
   Share now the human exile's woe.
Mourns not that forest felled, which took
         Three hundred years to grow?

Grieve not those meadows scarred and cleft,
   Mined with deep holes and reft of grass,
Gardens where not a flower is left,
         Fouled streams, once clear as glass?

And yon green vale where Spring was found
   Laughing among her daffodils . . .
Winds sweep it now; a battle-ground
         Between two gun-swept hills.

THE TENTH ARMISTICE DAY

I

'Lest we forget!' Let us remember, then,
   How England cheered – sang – shouted, in the glow

Of a fog-shrouded sun ten years ago;
How Peace rose, like a dim star on a fen.
And yet, so short the memories of men,
Do we indeed remember War laid low,
Peace brought, by one great man* at one great blow,
Dealt by one clarion voice and golden pen?

Surely his voice comes borne to us with theirs
Who fell – the voice of husband, brother, father,
Lover and son: 'Spend not on us your cares,
Your wreaths, for we have better flowers to gather.
But lift the load our workless comrade bears:
Flowers for the dead? Bread for the living rather!'

II

And yet bring flowers and heap them, all this day,
On the high Cenotaph, memorial-wise,
So to commemorate their sacrifice:
No flowers can be more beautiful than they.
Let the red rose of England burn alway,
And amaranth, for their life that never dies,
And poppies reddening round, where laurel lies
Also. Yet more they ask; yet more they may.

Give, give the pyramid its cope and crown
In the olive-leaf, the Peace dove's silver glitter,
Flying above the red flood's desolations!
They warred to end war: to fulfil their hope
Give them a better monument and fitter;
Build their memorial in the League of Nations!

*President Wilson.

Elizabeth Chandler Forman

THE THREE LADS

Down the road rides a German lad,
  Into the distance grey;
Straight toward the north as a bullet flies,
The dusky north, with its cold, sad skies;
But the song that he sings is merry and glad,
  For he's off to the war and away.
'Then hey! for our righteous king!' (he cries)
'And the good old God in his good old skies!
And ho! for love and a pair of blue eyes, –
  For I'm off to the war and away!'

Down the road rides a Russian lad,
  Into the distance grey,
Out toward the glare of the steppes he spurs,
And he hears the wolves in the southern firs;
But the song that he sings is blithe and glad,
  For he's off to the war and away.
'Then hey! for our noble tzar!' (he cries)
'And liberty that never dies!
And ho! for love and a pair of blue eyes, –
  For I'm off to the war and away!'

Down the road rides an English lad,
  Into the distance grey.
Through the murk and fog of the river's breath,
Through the dank, dark night he rides to his death;
But the song that he sings is gay and glad,
  For he's off to the war and away.
'Then hey! for our honest king!' (he cries)
'And hey! for truth, and down with lies!
And ho! for love and a pair of blue eyes, –
  For I'm off to the war and away!'

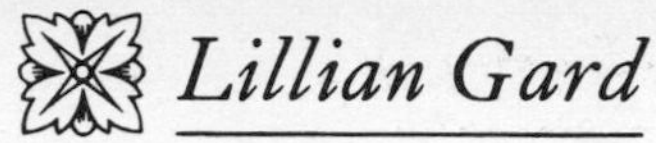

Lillian Gard

HER 'ALLOWANCE'!

'Er looked at me bunnet (I knows 'e ain't noo!)
'Er turned up 'er nose at the patch on me shoe!
And 'er sez, pointed like, 'Liza, what do 'e do
With yer 'llowance?'

'Er looked at the children (they'm clean and they'm neat,
But their clothes be as plain as the victuals they eat):
And 'er sez, 'Why not dress 'em up fine for a treat
With yer 'llowance?'

I sees 'er long feather and trimmy-up gown:
I sez, as I looks 'er quite square up and down,
'Do 'e think us keeps 'oliday 'ere in the town
With my 'llowance?

'Not likely!' I sez. And I bids 'er 'Good-day!'
And I kneels on the shabby old canvas to pray
For Bill, who's out fightin' such brave miles away.
(And I puts back a foo o' they coins for 'e may
Be needin' a part – may my Bill – who can say? –
Of my 'llowance!)

Muriel Elsie Graham

THE LARK ABOVE THE TRENCHES

'A French soldier writing to *Le Matin* says that the other day a lark sang above the trenches its spring song, which was to them a song of joy and hope.' – *February 1915*

All day the guns had worked their hellish will,
And all night long
With sobbing breath men gasped their lives away,
Or shivered restless on the ice-cold clay,
Till morn broke pale and chill
With sudden song.

Above the sterile furrows war had ploughed
With deep-trenched seams,
Wherein this year such bitter seed is sown,
Wherein this year no fruitful grain is strown,
A lark poured from the cloud
Its throbbing dreams.

It sang – and pain and death were passing shows –
So glad and strong;
Life soared triumphant, though a myriad men
Were swept like leaves beyond the living's ken,
That wounded hope arose
To greet that song.

THE BATTLE OF THE SWAMPS

Across the blinded lowlands the beating rain blows chill,
The trenched earth turns to water, the shell-holes ooze and fill,
A tragic land where little that's sweet or sane survives –
O hungry swamps of Flanders that swallow up men's lives!

O numbing nights of Flanders, whose cold breath cannot quench
The grim enduring courage that holds each mud-fouled trench,
That struggles stiffly forward to meet the shattering guns –
O bitter swamps of Flanders that rob us of our sons!

Yet in the sheltered homeland that lies such worlds away,
What shrinking hearts are braving that suffocating clay!
And when on roof and window the rain beats, then – O then,
O deathless swamps of Flanders, our hearts are with our men.

Nora Griffiths

THE WYKHAMIST

In the wake of the yellow sunset one pale star
Hangs over the darkening city's purple haze.
An errand-boy in the street beneath me plays
On a penny whistle. Very faint and far
Comes the scroop of tortured gear on a battered car.
A hyacinth nods pallid blooms on the window sill,
Swayed by the tiny wind. St Catherine's Hill
Is a place of mystery, a land of dreams.
The tramp of soldiers, barrack-marching, seems
A thing remote, untouched by fate or time.
. . . A year ago you heard Cathedral's chime,
You hurried up to books – a year ago;
– Shouted for 'Houses' in New Field below.
. . . You . . . 'died of wounds' . . . they told me

. . . yet your feet
Pass with the others down the twilit street.

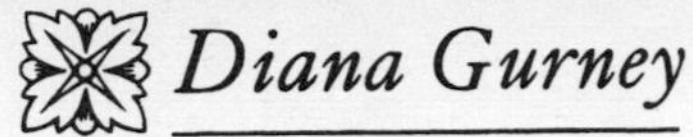

Diana Gurney

THE FALLEN

Shall we not lay our holly wreath
Here at the foot of this high cross?
We do not know, perhaps a breath
Of our remembering may come
To them at last where they are sleeping,
They are quiet, they are dumb,
No more of mirth, no more of weeping,
Silent Christmas they are keeping;
Ours the sorrow, ours the loss.

Cicely Hamilton

NON-COMBATANT

Before one drop of angry blood was shed
  I was sore hurt and beaten to my knee;
Before one fighting man reeled back and died
  The War-Lords struck at me.

They struck me down – an idle, useless mouth,
  As cumbrous – nay, more cumbrous – than the dead,
With life and heart afire to give and give
  I take a dole instead.

With life and heart afire to give and give
  I take and eat the bread of charity.
In all the length of all this eager land,
  No man has need of me.

That is my hurt – my burning, beating wound;
  That is the spear-thrust driven through my pride!
With aimless hands, and mouth that must be fed,
  I wait and stand aside.

Let me endure it, then, with stiffened lip:
  I, even I, have suffered in the strife!
Let me endure it then – I give my pride
  Where others give a life.

Helen Hamilton

THE GHOULS

You strange old ghouls,
Who gloat with dulled old eyes,
   Over those lists,
   Those dreadful lists,
   To see what name
   Of friend, relation,
   However distant,
   May be appended
To your private Roll of Honour.
Unknowingly you draw, it seems,
   From their young bodies,
   Dead young bodies,
   Fresh life,
   New value,
Now that yours are ebbing.
   You strange old ghouls,
Who gloat with dulled old eyes,
   Over those lists,
   Those dreadful lists,
   Of young men dead.

THE JINGO-WOMAN

Jingo-woman
(How I dislike you!)
Dealer in white feathers,
Insulter, self-appointed,
Of all the men you meet,
Not dressed in uniform,
When to your mind,
         (A sorry mind),
         They should be,
         The test?
The judgment of your eye,
That wild, infuriate eye,

Whose glance, so you declare,
        Reveals unerringly,
Who's good for military service.
Oh! exasperating woman,
I'd like to wring your neck,
        I really would!
        You make all women seem such duffers!
        Besides exemptions,
        Enforced and held reluctantly,
        – Not that you'll believe it –
        You *must* know surely
Men there are, and young men too,
Physically not fit to serve,
Who look in their civilian garb
        Quite stout and hearty.
And most of whom, I'll wager,
Have been rejected several times.
How keen, though, your delight,
        Keen and malignant,
Should one offer you his seat,
        In crowded bus or train,
Thus giving you the chance to say,
In cold, incisive tones of scorn:
        'No, I much prefer to stand
        As you, young man, are not in khaki!'
Heavens! I wonder you're alive!
        Oh, these men,
These twice-insulted men,
        What iron self-control they show.
        What wonderful forbearance!

But still the day may come
For you to prove yourself
As sacrificial as upbraiding.
So far they are not taking us
But if the war goes on much longer
        They might,

Nay more,
They must,
When the last man has gone.
And if and when that dark day dawns,
You'll join up first, of course,
Without waiting to be fetched.
But in the meantime,
Do hold your tongue!
You shame us women.
Can't you see it isn't decent,
To flout and goad men into doing,
What is not asked of you?

THE ROMANCING POET

Granted that you write verse,
Much better verse than I,
(Which isn't saying much!)
I wish you would refrain
From making glad romance
Of this most hideous war.
It has no glamour,
Save man's courage,
His indomitable spirit,
His forgetfulness of self!
If you have words –
Fit words, I mean,
Not your usual stock-in-trade,
Of tags and *clichés* –
To hymn such greatness,
Use them.
But have you?
Anyone can babble.
If you must wax descriptive,
Do get the background right,
A little right!

Helen Hamilton

The blood, the filth, the horrors,
Suffering on such a scale,
That you and I, try as we may,
        Can only faintly vision it.
Don't make a pretty song about it!
        It is an insult to the men,
        Doomed to be crucified each day,
        For us at home!
Abstain too, if you can,
From bidding us to plume ourselves
For being of the self-same breed
        As these heroic souls,
With the obvious implication,
We have the right to take the credit,
        Vicarious credit,
        For their immortal deeds!
        What next?
        It is an outrage!
        We are not glory-snatchers!

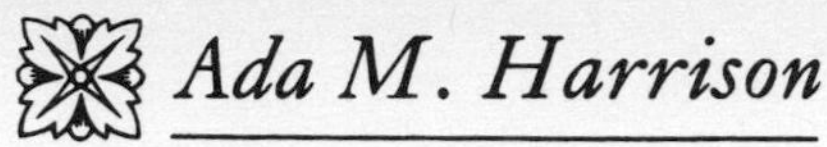

NEW YEAR, 1916

Those that go down into silence . . .

There is no silence in their going down,
   Although their grave-turf is not wet with tears,
Although Grief passes by them, and Renown
   Has garnered them no glory for the years.

The cloud of war moves on, and men forget
   That empires fall. We go our heedless ways
Unknowing still, uncaring still, and yet
   The very dust is clamorous with their praise.

Mary H. J. Henderson

AN INCIDENT

He was just a boy, as I could see,
For he sat in the tent there close by me.
I held the lamp with its flickering light,
And felt the hot tears blur my sight
As the doctor took the blood-stained bands
From both his brave, shell-shattered hands –
His boy hands, wounded more pitifully
Than Thine, O Christ, on Calvary.

I was making tea in the tent where they,
The wounded, came in their agony;
And the boy turned when his wounds were dressed,
Held up his face like a child at the breast,
Turned and held his tired face up,
For he could not hold the spoon or cup,
And I fed him. . . . Mary, Mother of God,
All women tread where thy feet have trod.

And still on the battlefield of pain
Christ is stretched on His Cross again;
And the Son of God in agony hangs,
Womanhood striving to ease His pangs.
For each son of man is a son divine,
Not just to the mother who calls him 'mine',
As he stretches out his stricken hand,
Wounded to death for the Mother Land.

Agnes Grozier Herbertson

AIRMAN, R.F.C.

He heard them in the silence of the night
Whirring and thudding through the moonlit sky
And wondered where their target, pondered why . . .
Unsleeping, saw again with a young sight
The docks, yards, aerodromes revealed and white,
Heard the guns crack, saw searchlights sidle by,
Felt the bombs fall, the débris mounting high,
Knew the earth blazing and the skies alight . . .

They had his task; they did what he had done:
Their youth – as his – by battle was hemmed round:
Their lives hung on a thread – how finely spun! –
(Little they cared as on their way they wound!) . . .
He prayed they might come safely through, each one,
And find a better world than he had found.

THE SEED-MERCHANT'S SON

The Seed-Merchant has lost his son,
His dear, his loved, his only one.

So young he was. Even now it seems
He was a child with a child's dreams.

He would race over the meadow-bed
With his bright, bright eyes and his cheeks all red.

Fair and healthy and long of limb:
It made one young just to look at him.

His school books, into the cupboard thrust,
Have scarcely had time to gather dust.

Died in the war. . . . And it seems his eyes
Must have looked at death with a child's surprise.

. . .

Agnes Grozier Herbertson

The Seed-Merchant goes on his way:
I saw him out on his land today;

Old to have fathered so young a son,
And now the last glint of his youth is gone.

What could one say to him in his need?
Little there seemed to say indeed.

So still he was that the birds flew round
The grey of his head without a sound,

Careless and tranquil in the air,
As if naught human were standing there.

. . .

Oh, never a soul could understand
Why he looked at the earth, and the seed in his hand,

As he had never before seen seed or sod:
I heard him murmur: 'Thank God, thank God!'

May Herschel-Clarke

'FOR VALOUR'

Jest bronze – you wouldn't ever know,
To see it jest a-lying there,
It's really made o' golden hair,
And firm young flesh as white as snow.
No gold, nor none o' them art tones –
Only two 'ands and willing feet,
A sturdy form, a young 'eart's beat,
Two gay, bright eyes – jest blood and bones . . .
My blood and bones, *my* 'eart. . . . Ah! well,
They wrote to tell me it was fine
To see the way he laid that mine,
So brave and smiling . . . then he fell. . . .
There never was no 'olding 'im,
And there it must 'a' bin the same.
But, 'fore he . . . went . . . he called my name. . . .
Eh, but it makes my old eyes dim
To think I was so far away. . . .
Yes, that's 'is photo. Look at it.
Say, don't you think I've done my bit? . . .
Jest bronze. . . . *Gawd! What a price to pay!*

'NOTHING TO REPORT'

One minute we was laughin', me an' Ted,
The next, he lay beside me grinnin' – dead.
'There's nothin' to report,' the papers said.

Teresa Hooley

A WAR FILM

I saw,
With a catch of the breath and the heart's uplifting,
Sorrow and pride,
   The 'week's great draw' –
The Mons Retreat;
The 'Old Contemptibles' who fought, and died,
The horror and the anguish and the glory.

As in a dream,
Still hearing machine-guns rattle and shells scream,
I came out into the street.

When the day was done,
My little son
Wondered at bath-time why I kissed him so,
Naked upon my knee.
How could he know
The sudden terror that assaulted me? . . .
The body I had borne
Nine moons beneath my heart,
A part of me . . .
If, someday,
It should be taken away
To War. Tortured. Torn.
Slain.
Rotting in No Man's Land, out in the rain –
My little son . . .
Yet all those men had mothers, every one.

How should he know
Why I kissed and kissed and kissed him, crooning his name?
He thought that I was daft.
He thought it was a game,
And laughed, and laughed.

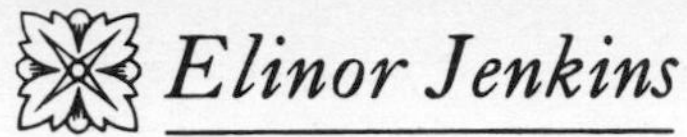

Elinor Jenkins

DULCE ET DECORUM?

We buried of our dead the dearest one –
Said each to other, 'Here then let him lie,
And they may find the place, when all is done,
From the old may tree standing guard near by.'

Strong limbs whereon the wasted life blood dries,
And soft cheeks that a girl might wish her own,
A scholar's brow, o'ershadowing valiant eyes,
Henceforth shall pleasure charnel-worms alone.

For we, that loved him, covered up his face,
And laid him in the sodden earth away,
And left him lying in that lonely place
To rot and moulder with the mouldering clay.

The hawthorn that above his grave head grew
Like an old crone toward the raw earth bowed,
Wept softly over him, the whole night through,
And made him of her tears a glimmering shroud.

. . .

Oh Lord of Hosts, no hallowed prayer we bring,
Here for Thy grace is no importuning,
No room for those that will not strive nor cry
When lovingkindness with our dead lies slain:
  Give us our fathers' heathen hearts again,
  Valour to dare, and fortitude to die.

REPORTED MISSING

My thought shall never be that you are dead:
Who laughed so lately in this quiet place.
The dear and deep-eyed humour of that face
Held something ever living, in Death's stead.
Scornful I hear the flat things they have said
And all their piteous platitudes of pain.
I laugh! I laugh! – For you will come again –
This heart would never beat if you were dead.
The world's adrowse in twilight hushfulness,
There's purple lilac in your little room,
And somewhere out beyond the evening gloom
Small boys are culling summer watercress.
Of these familiar things I have no dread
Being so very sure you are not dead.

Margery Lawrence

THE LOST ARMY

'The 1/5 Norfolks . . . consisting of 16 officers and 250 men . . . charged into a wood . . . not one of them came out again.'
Sir Ian Hamilton's Suvla Bay despatch, 1916

Singing and shouting they swept to the treacherous forest
Darkness and silence received them and smothered their pain
Darkness and silence and night is the end of their story –
They came not again!

Never a hero came forth of the legions that entered
Never a cry nor a prayer, nor a song of the brave
Dark and in silence the sinister forest received them
And made them a grave!

Somewhere deep down in the heart of the wood that betrayed them
Shoulder to shoulder they lie, with their wounds to the fore
There in the dark and the silence they sleep, the Lost Army
Returning no more.

We may not hear of their valour, their death or their glory
Nay! They were ours – and they died for their country, and so
Darkness and silence and night is the end of their story –
All we need know.

1916

TRANSPORT OF WOUNDED IN MESOPOTAMIA, 1917

You who sat safe at home
And let us die
You who said 'all was well'
And knew the lie. . . .
(Fever and flies and sand
Sand and fever and flies
Till the end of each weary day
Saw the wearier night arise!)

Margery Lawrence

You who sat safe at home
And let us die!

Sun in our hopeless eyes
As the crawling barges plied
On the waveless, treacly tide –
(Sand and fever and flies
Flies and fever and sand
Till we smiled at our good friend Death
When he shook us by the hand!)
When we dreamt of rest and care –
But the mirage flitted away
And day after tortured day
Closed – in the same despair!

Hush, and bury it deep –
Bury us side by side!
Shuffle the cards again
Juggle – 'regret' and 'explain' –
You – for whose fault we died!

We who lie far away
God! Hear our cry
Upon Their hands our blood
Is yet undry
Those who sat safe at Home
And let us die!

Winifred M. Letts

CASUALTY

John Delaney of the Rifles has been shot.
   A man we never knew,
   Does it cloud the day for you
   That he lies among the dead
Moving, hearing, heeding not?

No history will hold his humble name.
   No sculptured stone will tell
   The traveller where he fell;
   That he lies among the dead
Is the measure of his fame.

When our troops return victorious shall we care
   That deaf to all the cheers,
   Lacking tribute of our tears,
   He is lying with the dead
Stark and silent, God knows where?

John Delaney of the Rifles – who was he?
   A name seen on a list
   All unknown and all unmissed.
   What to us that he is dead? –
Yet he died for you and me.

THE DESERTER

There was a man, – don't mind his name,
Whom Fear had dogged by night and day.
He could not face the German guns
And so he turned and ran away.
Just that – he turned and ran away,
But who can judge him, you or I?
God makes a man of flesh and blood
Who yearns to live and not to die.
And this man when he feared to die
Was scared as any frightened child,

His knees were shaking under him,
His breath came fast, his eyes were wild.
I've seen a hare with eyes as wild,
With throbbing heart and sobbing breath.
But oh! it shames one's soul to see
A man in abject fear of death.
But fear had gripped him, so had death;
His number had gone up that day,
They might not heed his frightened eyes,
They shot him when the dawn was grey.
Blindfolded, when the dawn was grey,
He stood there in a place apart,
The shots rang out and down he fell,
An English bullet in his heart.
An English bullet in his heart!
But here's the irony of life, –
His mother thinks he fought and fell
A hero, foremost in the strife.
So she goes proudly; to the strife
Her best, her hero son she gave.
O well for her she does not know
He lies in a deserter's grave.

SCREENS

(In a Hospital)

They put the screens around his bed;
  A crumpled heap I saw him lie,
White counterpane and rough dark head,
  Those screens – they showed that he would die.

They put the screens about his bed;
  We might not play the gramophone,
And so we played at cards instead
  And left him dying there alone.

The covers on the screen are red,
   The counterpanes are white and clean; –
He might have lived and loved and wed
   But now he's done for at nineteen.

An ounce or more of Turkish lead,
   He got his wounds at Suvla Bay;
They've brought the Union Jack to spread
   Upon him when he goes away.

He'll want those three red screens no more,
   Another man will get his bed,
We'll make the row we did before
   But – Jove! – I'm sorry that he's dead.

WHAT REWARD?

You gave your life, boy,
   And *you* gave a limb:
But he who gave his precious wits,
   Say, what reward for him?

One has his glory,
   One has found his rest.
But what of this poor babbler here
   With chin sunk on his breast?

Flotsam of battle,
   With brain bemused and dim,
O God, for such a sacrifice
   Say, what reward for him?

Olive E. Lindsay

DESPAIR

Half of me died at Bapaume,
  And the rest of me is a log:
For my soul was in the other half;
  And the half that is here is a clog
On the one who would always be doing
  In days never to come again.
Carry me into the darkness, sir,
  And put me out of my pain.

The best of me died at Bapaume
  When the world went up in fire,
And the soul that was mine deserted
  And left me, a thing in the mire,
With a madden'd and dim remembrance
  Of a time when my life was whole.
Carry me into the darkness, sir,
  And let me find my soul.

If half of you went at Bapaume,
  And with it your soul went too,
That soul has laid as a sacrifice
  The half that was torn from you.
At the feet of the One who Himself has given,
  Laid all that a man can give;
And then will return to the other half
  And show it how to live.

Amy Lowell

CONVALESCENCE

From out the dragging vastness of the sea,
  Wave-fettered, bound in sinuous seaweed strands,
  He toils toward the rounding beach, and stands
One moment, white and dripping, silently,
Cut like a cameo in lazuli,
  Then falls, betrayed by shifting shells, and lands
  Prone in the jeering water, and his hands
Clutch for support where no support can be.
  So up, and down, and forward, inch by inch,
He gains upon the shore, where poppies glow
And sandflies dance their little lives away.
  The sucking waves retard, and tighter clinch
The weeds about him, but the land-winds blow,
And in the sky there blooms the sun of May.

Rose Macaulay

PICNIC

July 1917

We lay and ate sweet hurt-berries
  In the bracken of Hurt Wood.
Like a quire of singers singing low
  The dark pines stood.

Behind us climbed the Surrey hills,
  Wild, wild in greenery;
At our feet the downs of Sussex broke
  To an unseen sea.

And life was bound in a still ring,
  Drowsy, and quiet, and sweet . . .
When heavily up the south-east wind
  The great guns beat.

We did not wince, we did not weep,
  We did not curse or pray;
We drowsily heard, and someone said,
  'They sound clear today'.

We did not shake with pity and pain,
  Or sicken and blanch white.
We said, 'If the wind's from over there
  There'll be rain tonight'.

. . .

Once pity we knew, and rage we knew,
  And pain we knew, too well,
As we stared and peered dizzily
  Through the gates of hell.

But now hell's gates are an old tale;
  Remote the anguish seems;
The guns are muffled and far away,
  Dreams within dreams.

And far and far are Flanders mud,
  And the pain of Picardy;
And the blood that runs there runs beyond
  The wide waste sea.

We are shut about by guarding walls:
  (We have built them lest we run
Mad from dreaming of naked fear
  And of black things done).

We are ringed all round by guarding walls,
  So high, they shut the view.
Not all the guns that shatter the world
  Can quite break through.

. . .

Oh, guns of France, oh, guns of France,
  Be still, you crash in vain. . . .
Heavily up the south wind throb
  Dull dreams of pain, . . .

Be still, be still, south wind, lest your
  Blowing should bring the rain. . . .
We'll lie very quiet on Hurt Hill,
  And sleep once again.

Oh, we'll lie quite still, nor listen nor look,
  While the earth's bounds reel and shake,
Lest, battered too long, our walls and we
  Should break . . . should break. . . .

THE SHADOW

There was a Shadow on the moon; I saw it poise and tilt, and go
Its lonely way, and so I know that the blue velvet night will soon
Blaze loud and bright, as if the stars were crashing right into the town,
And tumbling streets and houses down, and smashing people like wine-jars. . . .

Fear wakes:
What then?
Strayed shadow of the Fear that breaks
The world's young men.

Bright fingers point all round the sky, they point and grope and cannot find.
(God's hand, you'd think, and he gone blind.) . . . The queer white faces twist and cry.
Last time they came they messed our square, and left it a hot rubbish-heap,
With people sunk in it so deep, you could not even hear them swear.

Fire blinds.
What then?
Pale shadow of the Pain that grinds
The world's young men.

The weak blood running down the street, oh, does it run like fire, like wine?
Are the spilt brains so keen, so fine, crushed limbs so swift, dead dreams so sweet?
There is a Plain where limbs and dreams and brains to set the world a-fire
Lie tossed in sodden heaps of mire. . . . Crash! Tonight's show begins, it seems.

Death . . . Well,
What then?
Rim of the shadow of the Hell
Of the world's young men.

Nina Macdonald

SING A SONG OF WAR-TIME

Sing a song of War-time,
Soldiers marching by,
Crowds of people standing,
Waving them 'Good-bye'.
When the crowds are over,
Home we go to tea,
Bread and margarine to eat,
War economy!

If I ask for cake, or
Jam of any sort,
Nurse says, 'What! in War-time?
Archie, cert'nly not!'
Life's not very funny
Now, for little boys,
Haven't any money,
Can't buy any toys.

Mummie does the house-work,
Can't get any maid,
Gone to make munitions,
'Cause they're better paid,
Nurse is always busy,
Never time to play,
Sewing shirts for soldiers,
Nearly ev'ry day.

Ev'ry body's doing
Something for the War,
Girls are doing things
They've never done before,
Go as 'bus conductors,
Drive a car or van,
All the world is topsy-turvy
Since the War began.

Florence Ripley Mastin

AT THE MOVIES

They swing across the screen in brave array,
  Long British columns grinding the dark grass.
Twelve months ago they marched into the grey
  Of battle; yet again behold them pass!

One lifts his dusty cap; his hair is bright;
  I meet his eyes, eager and young and bold.
The picture quivers into ghostly white;
  Then I remember, and my heart grows cold!

January, 1916

Charlotte Mew

THE CENOTAPH

September 1919

Not yet will those measureless fields be green again
Where only yesterday the wild sweet blood of wonderful youth was shed;
There is a grave whose earth must hold too long, too deep a stain,
Though for ever over it we may speak as proudly as we may tread.
But here, where the watchers by lonely hearths from the thrust of an inward sword have more slowly bled,
We shall build the Cenotaph: Victory, winged, with Peace, winged too, at the column's head.
And over the stairway, at the foot – oh! here, leave desolate, passionate hands to spread
Violets, roses, and laurel, with the small, sweet, twinkling country things
Speaking so wistfully of other Springs,
From the little gardens of little places where son or sweetheart was born and bred.
In splendid sleep, with a thousand brothers
To lovers – to mothers
Here, too, lies he:
Under the purple, the green, the red,
It is all young life: it must break some women's hearts to see
Such a brave, gay coverlet to such a bed!
Only, when all is done and said,
God is not mocked and neither are the dead.
For this will stand in our Market-place –
Who'll sell, who'll buy
(Will you or I
Lie each to each with the better grace)?
While looking into every busy whore's and huckster's face
As they drive their bargains, is the Face
Of God: and some young, piteous, murdered face.

MAY, 1915

Let us remember Spring will come again
To the scorched, blackened woods, where the wounded trees
Wait with their old wise patience for the heavenly rain,
Sure of the sky: sure of the sea to send its healing breeze,
Sure of the sun. And even as to these
Surely the Spring, when God shall please,
Will come again like a divine surprise
To those who sit today with their great Dead, hands in their hands, eyes in their eyes,
At one with Love, at one with Grief: blind to the scattered things and changing skies.

JUNE, 1915

Who thinks of June's first rose today?
Only some child, perhaps, with shining eyes and rough bright hair will reach it down
In a green sunny lane, to us almost as far away
As are the fearless stars from these veiled lamps of town.
What's little June to a great broken world with eyes gone dim
From too much looking on the face of grief, the face of dread?
Or what's the broken world to June and him
Of the small eager hand, the shining eyes, the rough bright head?

Alice Meynell

'LORD, I OWE THEE A DEATH'

(Richard Hooker)

Man pays that debt with new munificence,
  Not piecemeal now, not slowly, by the old:
Not grudgingly, by the effaced thin pence,
  But greatly and in gold.

SUMMER IN ENGLAND, 1914

On London fell a clearer light;
  Caressing pencils of the sun
Defined the distances, the white
  Houses transfigured one by one,
The 'long, unlovely street' impearled.
O what a sky has walked the world!

Most happy year! And out of town
  The hay was prosperous, and the wheat;
The silken harvest climbed the down:
  Moon after moon was heavenly-sweet,
Stroking the bread within the sheaves,
Looking 'twixt apples and their leaves.

And while this rose made round her cup,
  The armies died convulsed. And when
This chaste young silver sun went up
  Softly, a thousand shattered men,
One wet corruption, heaped the plain,
After a league-long throb of pain.

Flower following tender flower; and birds,
  And berries; and benignant skies
Made thrive the serried flocks and herds. –
  Yonder are men shot through the eyes.
        Love, hide thy face
From man's unpardonable race.

. . .

Who said 'No man hath greater love than this,
   To die to serve his friend'?
So these have loved us all unto the end.
   Chide thou no more, O thou unsacrificed!
The soldier dying dies upon a kiss,
   The very kiss of Christ.

Ruth Comfort Mitchell

HE WENT FOR A SOLDIER

He marched away with a blithe young score of him
  With the first volunteers,
Clear-eyed and clean and sound to the core of him,
  Blushing under the cheers.
They were fine, new flags that swung a-flying there,
Oh, the pretty girls he glimpsed a-crying there,
  Pelting him with pinks and with roses –
  Billy, the Soldier Boy!

Not very clear in the kind young heart of him
  What the fuss was about,
But the flowers and the flags seemed part of him –
  The music drowned his doubt.
It's a fine, brave sight they were a-coming there
To the gay, bold tune they kept a-drumming there,
  While the boasting fifes shrilled jauntily –
  Billy, the Soldier Boy!

Soon he is one with the blinding smoke of it –
  Volley and curse and groan:
Then he has done with the knightly joke of it –
  It's rending flesh and bone.
There are pain-crazed animals a-shrieking there
And a warm blood stench that is a-reeking there;
  He fights like a rat in a corner –
  Billy, the Soldier Boy!

There he lies now, like a ghoulish score of him,
  Left on the field for dead:
The ground all around is smeared with the gore of him –
  Even the leaves are red.
The Thing that was Billy lies a-dying there,
Writhing and a-twisting and a-crying there;
  A sickening sun grins down on him –
  Billy, the Soldier Boy!

Still not quite clear in the poor, wrung heart of him
  What the fuss was about,

Ruth Comfort Mitchell

See where he lies – or a ghastly part of him –
   While life is oozing out:
There are loathsome things he sees a-crawling there;
There are hoarse-voiced crows he hears a-calling there,
   Eager for the foul feast spread for them –
   Billy, the Soldier Boy!

How much longer, O Lord, shall we bear it all?
   How many more red years?
Story it and glory it and share it all,
   In seas of blood and tears?
They are braggart attitudes we've worn so long;
They are tinsel platitudes we've sworn so long –
   We who have turned the Devil's Grindstone,
   Borne with the hell called War!

Harriet Monroe

ON THE PORCH

As I lie roofed in, screened in,
From the pattering rain,
The summer rain –
As I lie
Snug and dry,
And hear the birds complain:

Oh, billow on billow,
Oh, roar on roar,
Over me wash
The seas of war.
Over me – down – down –
Lunges and plunges
The huge gun with its one blind eye,
The armoured train,
And, swooping out of the sky,
The aeroplane.
Down – down –
The army proudly swinging
Under gay flags,
The glorious dead heaped up like rags,
A church with bronze bells ringing,
A city all towers,
Gardens of lovers and flowers,
The round world swinging
In the light of the sun:
All broken, undone,
All down – under
Black surges of thunder . . .

Oh, billow on billow
Oh, roar on roar,
Over me wash
The seas of war . . .

As I lie roofed in, screened in,
From the pattering rain,

Harriet Monroe

The summer rain –
As I lie
Snug and dry,
And hear the birds complain.

Edith Nesbit

THE FIELDS OF FLANDERS

Last year the fields were all glad and gay
With silver daisies and silver may;
There were kingcups gold by the river's edge
And primrose stars under every hedge.

This year the fields are trampled and brown,
The hedges are broken and beaten down,
And where the primroses used to grow
Are little black crosses set in a row.

And the flower of hopes, and the flowers of dreams,
The noble, fruitful, beautiful schemes,
The tree of life with its fruit and bud,
Are trampled down in the mud and the blood.

The changing seasons will bring again
The magic of Spring to our wood and plain:
Though the Spring be so green as never was seen
The crosses will still be black in the green.

The God of battles shall judge the foe
Who trampled our country and laid her low. . . .
God! hold our hands on the reckoning day,
Lest all we owe them we should repay.

1915

SPRING IN WAR-TIME

Now the sprinkled blackthorn snow
   Lies along the lovers' lane
Where last year we used to go –
   Where we shall not go again.

In the hedge the buds are new,
   By our wood the violets peer –
Just like last year's violets, too,
   But they have no scent this year.

Every bird has heart to sing
 Of its nest, warmed by its breast;
We had heart to sing last spring,
 But we never built our nest.

Presently red roses blown
 Will make all the garden gay. . . .
Not yet have the daisies grown
 On your clay.

1916

Eileen Newton

LAST LEAVE

(1918)

Let us forget tomorrow! For tonight
At least, with curtains drawn, and driftwood piled
On our own hearthstone, we may rest, and see
The firelight flickering on familiar walls.
(How the blue flames leap when an ember falls!)
Peace, and content, and soul-security –
These are within. Without, the waste is wild
With storm-clouds sweeping by in furious flight,
And ceaseless beating of autumnal rain
Upon our window pane.

The dusk grows deeper now, the flames are low:
We do not heed the shadows, you and I,
Nor fear the grey wings of encroaching gloom,
So softly they enfold us. One last gleam
Flashes and flits, elusive as a dream,
And then dies out upon the darkened room.
So, even so, our earthly fires must die;
Yet, in our hearts, love's flame shall leap and glow
When this dear night, with all it means to me,
Is but a memory!

REVISION

(For November 11th)

In those two silent moments, when we stand
To let the surging tide of memory fill
The mind's deep caverns with its mingled flood
Of joys and griefs, I shall not think again,
As I was wont, of the untimely slain,
Of poppies dipped and dyed in human blood,
Of the rude cross upon the ravaged hill,
And all the strife which scarred that lovely land.

My thoughts shall seek, instead, a hallowed place –
The little, leafy wood where you and I
Spent the last hour together, while the breeze
Lulled every nodding daffodil to rest;
And from the flaming ramparts of the west
Shone bars of gold between black stems of trees,
Till dusk crept softly down the April sky,
And Hesperus trembled in the sapphire space.

Remembering this, my heart, at length set free
From gyves of hate, its bitter passion shed,
May hear once more the low, caressing call
That so entranced it, seven sad years ago.
Then, in those poignant moments, I shall know
That pain and parting matter not at all,
Because your soul, long-risen from the dead,
Is crowned by love's immortal constancy.

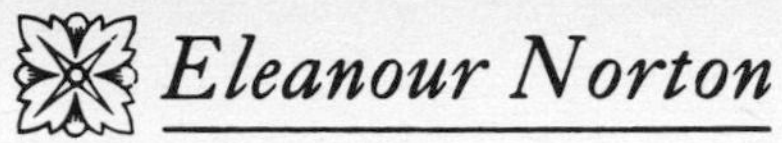

Eleanour Norton

IN A RESTAURANT, 1917

Encircled by the traffic's roar
Midst music and the blaze of light,
The battle-jaded khaki knights
Throng, sleek and civilised once more.

Oh, one there was who, long ago
(Three centuries or is it years?)
Adored the splendour and the tears
Of London Ebb – of London Flow.

Oh, one whose very presence gave
The common air an added grace,
Now in our hearts an empty place
And far in France an unmarked grave.

Carola Oman

AMBULANCE TRAIN 30

A.T. 30 lies in the siding.
Above her cold grey clouds lie, silver-long as she.
Like a great battleship that never saw defeat
She dreams: while the pale day dies down
Behind the harbour town,
Beautiful, complete
And unimpassioned as the long grey sea.

A.T. 30 lies in the siding.
Gone are her red crosses – the sick that were her own.
Like a great battleship that never saw defeat
She waits, while the pale day dies down
Behind the harbour town,
Beautiful, complete. . . .
And the Occupying Army boards her for Cologne.

May 6, 1919

BRUSSELS, 1919

Wide are the streets, and driven clean
With slanting rain. Behind tall gates
The lilac trees shoot silver green.
The boulevards sing with traffic. Still
The arches triumph on each hill.
And the victorious city waits
But for her soldiers' homecoming.

The shops are bright in fresh array.
The tramcars ring and jangle by
Crowded with soldiers. Every day
Brings home to her more exiled sons –
Dawns grey upon more captured guns –
And just outside the city lie
Her forests, warm with welcoming. . . .

A mile or two outside the town
The silent forests stand; that spread

Down where the road has faded brown
And the pale leaves fall silver red,
Thick underfoot in rise and swell
Damp with old rains and sweet to smell,
Red underfoot, red overhead.

The road is white beneath the moon.
Go on until the dawn is new,
And you may meet the strange dragoon
And he may stop to ride with you.
(His men have faces pale as smoke,
But understand an English joke
Upon the road to Waterloo.)

May O'Rourke

THE MINORITY: 1917

She curls her darkened lashes; manicures
Her scented hands; rubs cream where by and by
The tell-tale lines will gather. –
                                        She is yours,
O Dead! who went to die

To save her light blue eyes from dreadful scenes,
To keep her dainty feet from broken ways,
Her youth from Hell – now see her as she preens
Bright thro' the weary days,

Tinkling her silly mirth against the dread
Calm of those lives who listen for dear feet
That will not come again.
                                        – Ah! fool! you tread
No mere commercial street,

But ground made consecrate by their spilt lives
Who stood but yesterday where now you stand
And died; or grope in darkness; fret in gyves,
Or lack their good right hand;

Or stare with dark and witless eyes that brood
Dumbly, upon the panic of an hour
When all the world was red.

                                        – And *you* are hued
Gay, as a painted flower,
Filling our days with foolishness and noise
And wooing Love with all your careful arts,
Forgetting quite the thousand, thousand boys
Who gave you their pierced hearts!

Emily Orr

A RECRUIT FROM THE SLUMS

'What has your country done for you,
   Child of a city slum,
That you should answer her ringing call
To man the gap and keep the wall
And hold the field though a thousand fall
   And help be slow to come?

'What has your country given to you,
   Her poor relation and friend?'
'Oh, a fight like death for your board and keep,
And some pitiful silver coins per week
   And the thought of the "house" at the end.'

'What can your country ask from you,
   Dregs of the British race?'
'She gave us little, she taught us less,
And why we were born we could hardly guess
Till we felt the surge of battle press
   And looked the foe in the face.'

'Greater love hath no man than this
   That a man should die for his friend.'
'We thought life cruel, and England cold;
But our bones were made from the English mould,
And when all is said, she's our mother old
   And we creep to her breast at the end.'

Jessie Pope

THE CALL

Who's for the trench –
  Are you, my laddie?
Who'll follow French –
  Will you, my laddie?
Who's fretting to begin,
Who's going out to win?
And who wants to save his skin –
  Do you, my laddie?

Who's for the khaki suit –
  Are you, my laddie?
Who longs to charge and shoot –
  Do you, my laddie?
Who's keen on getting fit,
Who means to show his grit,
And who'd rather wait a bit –
  Would you, my laddie?

Who'll earn the Empire's thanks –
  Will you, my laddie?
Who'll swell the victor's ranks –
  Will you, my laddie?
When that procession comes,
Banners and rolling drums –
Who'll stand and bite his thumbs –
  Will you, my laddie?

THE NUT'S BIRTHDAY

When Gilbert's birthday came *last* spring,
  Oh! how our brains we racked
To try and find a single thing
  Our languid dear one lacked;
For, since he nestled at his ease
  Upon the lap of Plenty,
Stock birthday presents failed to please
  The Nut of two and twenty.

And so we bought, to suit his taste –
  Refined and dilettante –
Some ormolu, grotesquely chased;
  A little bronze Bacchante;
A flagon of the Stuarts' reign;
  A 'Corot' to content him.
Well, now his birthday's come again,
  And *this* is what we sent him:

Some candles and a bar of soap,
  Cakes, peppermints and matches,
A pot of jam, some thread (like rope)
  For stitching khaki patches.
These gifts, our soldier writes to say,
  Have brought him untold riches
To celebrate his natal day
  In hard-won Flanders' ditches.

SOCKS

Shining pins that dart and click
  In the fireside's sheltered peace
Check the thoughts that cluster thick –
  20 plain and then decrease.

He was brave – well, so was I –
  Keen and merry, but his lip
Quivered when he said good-bye –
  Purl the seam-stitch, purl and slip.

Never used to living rough,
  Lots of things he'd got to learn;
Wonder if he's warm enough –
  Knit 2, catch 2, knit 1, turn.

Hark! The paper-boys again!
  Wish that shout could be suppressed;
Keeps one always on the strain –
  Knit off 9, and slip the rest.

Wonder if he's fighting now,
What he's done an' where he's been;
He'll come out on top, somehow –
Slip 1, knit 2, purl 14.

WAR GIRLS

There's the girl who clips your ticket for the train,
And the girl who speeds the lift from floor to floor,
There's the girl who does a milk-round in the rain,
And the girl who calls for orders at your door.
Strong, sensible, and fit,
They're out to show their grit,
And tackle jobs with energy and knack.
No longer caged and penned up,
They're going to keep their end up
Till the khaki soldier boys come marching back.

There's the motor girl who drives a heavy van,
There's the butcher girl who brings your joint of meat,
There's the girl who cries 'All fares, please!' like a man,
And the girl who whistles taxis up the street.
Beneath each uniform
Beats a heart that's soft and warm,
Though of canny mother-wit they show no lack;
But a solemn statement this is,
They've no time for love and kisses
Till the khaki soldier boys come marching back.

Inez Quilter (Aged 11 years)

'SALL'

(In Aid of the Wounded Horses)

I'm none of yer London gentry,
None o' yer Hyde Park swells,
But I'm only a farmer's plough horse
And I'se born among hills and fells.

Yer mus'n't expect no graces
For yer won't get 'em from me,
I'se made as nature intended
An' I'm jus' plain Sall, d'ye see.

You've not seen me in the Row yet
An' yer won't, if yer try so 'ard,
I'm not a show 'orse yer forget
But I'm Sall, plain Sall, and Sall goes 'ard!

Dorothy Una Ratcliffe

REMEMBRANCE DAY IN THE DALES

It's a fine kind thought! And yet – I know
The Abbey's not where our Jack should lie,
With his sturdy love of a rolling sky;
            As a tiny child
He loved a sea that was grand and wild.
            God knows best!
Near-by the sea our Jack should rest.

And Willie – Willie our youngest born –
I fear that he might be lonesome, laid
Where the echoing, deep-voiced prayers are said, –
And yet the deep-voiced praying words
Reach God's heart too with the hymns of the birds.
            In His keep
On the edge of a wood our Will should sleep.
            God knows best!
But the years are long since the lads went west.

Ursula Roberts

THE CENOTAPH

The man in the Trilby hat has furtively shifted it;
The man with the clay pipe has pushed his fists deeper into his
pockets;
Beparcelled women are straining their necks
To stare.
Through the spattered windows of the omnibus
We see,
Dumb beneath the rain,
Marshalled by careful policemen,
Four behind four,
The relatives of dead heroes,
Clutching damp wreaths.
Within the omnibus there is silence
But for a sniff.
Then a plump woman speaks,
Softly, unquerulously:
'I wouldn't', she says,
'I wouldn't stand in a queue to have my feelings harrowed,
Not my*self*, I wouldn't.'
The omnibus swerves to the pavement,
And the plump woman
Prepares for equable departure.
'But there,' she adds unbitterly,
'I often think it wouldn't do
For us all to be alike.
There's some as can't,
But then, again,
There's some, you see,
As can.'
Beautiful,
Plump woman,
(Plump of mind as well as of body)
Beautiful is your tolerance
Of human idiosyncrasy.
When my impatient feet would tap in irritation,
When my breath would break out in abuse,

Ursula Roberts

When my scornful lips would frame themselves
(At the vices,
Or at the virtues,
Of my neighbours)
Into a sneer only half pitiful,
May I remember you
And murmur with serenity,
Without intensity,
Without virulence,
'I wouldn't,
Not myself,
But then, again,
There's some, you see,
As can'.

Margaret Sackville

A MEMORY

There was no sound at all, no crying in the village,
Nothing you would count as sound, that is, after the shells;
Only behind a wall the low sobbing of women,
The creaking of a door, a lost dog – nothing else.

Silence which might be felt, no pity in the silence,
Horrible, soft like blood, down all the blood-stained ways;
In the middle of the street two corpses lie unburied,
And a bayoneted woman stares in the market-place.

Humble and ruined folk – for these no pride of conquest,
Their only prayer: 'O! Lord, give us our daily bread!'
Not by the battle fires, the shrapnel are we haunted;
Who shall deliver us from the memory of these dead?

SACRAMENT

Before the Altar of the world in flower,
Upon whose steps thy creatures kneel in line,
We do beseech Thee in this wild Spring hour,
Grant us, O Lord, thy wine. But not this wine.

Helpless, we, praying by Thy shimmering seas,
Beside Thy fields, whence all the world is fed,
Thy little children clinging about Thy knees,
Cry: 'Grant us, Lord, Thy bread!' But not this bread.

This wine of awful sacrifice outpoured;
This bread of life – of human lives. The Press
Is overflowing, the Wine-Press of the Lord! . . .
Yet doth he tread the foaming grapes no less.

These stricken lands! The green time of the year
Has found them wasted by a purple flood,
Sodden and wasted everywhere, everywhere; –
Not all our tears may cleanse them from that blood.

Margaret Sackville

The earth is all too narrow for our dead,
   So many and each a child of ours – and Thine
This flesh (our flesh) crumbled away like bread,
   This blood (our blood) poured out like wine, like wine.

Aimee Byng Scott

JULY 1st, 1916

A soft grey mist,
Poppies flamed brilliant where the woodlands bend
Or straggling in amongst the ripening corn,
Green grass dew kist;
While distantly a lark's pure notes ascend,
Greeting the morn.

A shuddering night;
Flames, not of poppies, cleave the quivering air,
The corn is razed, the twisted trees are dead;
War in his might
Has passed; Nature lies prostrate there
Stunned by his tread.

May Sinclair

FIELD AMBULANCE IN RETREAT

Via Dolorosa, Via Sacra

I

A straight flagged road, laid on the rough earth,
A causeway of stone from beautiful city to city,
Between the tall trees, the slender, delicate trees,
Through the flat green land, by plots of flowers, by black canals
thick with heat.

II

The road-makers made it well
Of fine stone, strong for the feet of the oxen and of the great
Flemish horses,
And for the high wagons piled with corn from the harvest.
And the labourers are few;
They and their quiet oxen stand aside and wait
By the long road loud with the passing of the guns, the rush of
armoured cars, and the tramp of an army on the march
forward to battle;
And, where the piled corn-wagons went, our dripping
Ambulance carries home
Its red and white harvest from the fields.

III

The straight flagged road breaks into dust, into a thin white
cloud,
About the feet of a regiment driven back league by league,
Rifles at trail, and standards wrapped in black funeral cloths.
Unhasting, proud in retreat,
They smile as the Red Cross Ambulance rushes by.
(You know nothing of beauty and of desolation who have not seen
That smile of an army in retreat.)
They go: and our shining, beckoning danger goes with them,
And our joy in the harvests that we gathered in at nightfall in the
fields;
And like an unloved hand laid on a beating heart
Our safety weighs us down.

Safety hard and strange; stranger and yet more hard
As, league after dying league, the beautiful, desolate Land
Falls back from the intolerable speed of an Ambulance in retreat
On the sacred, dolorous Way.

Edith Sitwell

THE DANCERS

(During a Great Battle, 1916)

The floors are slippery with blood:
The world gyrates too. God is good
That while His wind blows out the light
For those who hourly die for us –
We still can dance, each night.

The music has grown numb with death –
But we will suck their dying breath,
The whispered name they breathed to chance,
To swell our music, make it loud
That we may dance, – may dance.

We are the dull blind carrion-fly
That dance and batten. Though God die
Mad from the horror of the light –
The light is mad, too, flecked with blood, –
We dance, we dance, each night.

Cicily Fox Smith

THE CONVALESCENT

We've billards, bowls an' tennis courts, we've teas an' motor-
rides;
We've concerts nearly every night, an' 'eaps o' things besides;
We've all the best of everything as much as we can eat –
But my 'eart – my 'eart's at 'ome in 'Enry Street.

I'm askin' Sister every day when I'll be fit to go;
'We must 'ave used you bad' (she says) 'you want to leave us so';
I says, 'I beg your pardon, Nurse, the place is 'ard to beat,
But my 'eart – my 'eart's at 'ome in 'Enry Street.'

The sheffoneer we saved to buy, the clock upon the wall,
The pictures an' the almanac, the china dogs an' all,
I've thought about it many a time, my little 'ome complete,
When in Flanders, far away from 'Enry Street.

It's 'elped me through the toughest times – an' some was middlin'
tough –
The 'ardest march was not so 'ard, the roughest not so rough;
It's 'elped me keep my pecker up in victory an' defeat,
Just to think about my 'ome in 'Enry Street.

There's several things I'd like to 'ave which 'ere I never see,
I'd like some chipped potatoes an' a kipper to my tea;
But most of all I'd like to feel the stones beneath my feet
Of the road that takes me 'ome to 'Enry Street.

They'll 'ave a little flag 'ung out – they'll 'ave the parlour gay
With crinkled paper all about, the same as Christmas Day,
An' out of all the neighbours' doors the 'eads 'll pop to greet
Me comin' wounded 'ome to 'Enry Street.

My missis – well, she'll cry a bit, an' laugh a bit between;
My kids 'll climb upon my knees – there's one I've never seen;
An' of all the days which I 'ave known there won't be one so sweet
As the one when I go 'ome to 'Enry Street.

Marie Carmichael Stopes

NIGHT ON THE SHORE

Northumberland. August 6th, 1914

A dusky owl in velvet moth-like flight,
With feathers spread on non-resistant air,
Wheels on its silent wings, brushing my cheek.
The circles of its course are interlaced
By chuckling seagull-flocks, whose wide white wings
Sweep down to settle on the bare-ribbed sand
Left rich with treasure by the distant tide.
The owl gyrates, a part of the soft air,
Then upright, solemn, on my lowly tent
Perches beside me with his eyes intent
As though upon Minerva's shoulder. He
And I together watch the waves of cloud
Which slowly break and ripple o'er the moon,
Silvering celestial foam from their frayed edge.
The dim ethereal curve of the wide sand
Is flecked with hard black shadows, heightening
The fairy mountains left there in their play
By little weary waves which slid away
To slumber, cradled by the green-haired rocks.
Through the still water star-reflections deck
The red anemones with diadems.
This cosmic peace the owl and I have shared
For a whole moon of deep experience.

. . .

Tonight the moonbeams break on bayonets
Sharpened and gleaming in hot eager hands.
Tonight the swift low rush of battleships
Throbs up and down the bay, waking the waves.
Tonight my sleep is challenged in my tent
By martial voices backed by gleaming steel.
Tonight young men from cities meet the stars
When scanning the horizon for their foes.
Tonight there thrills all round our peaceful shores

The pulsing chain of men who wait on war.
And War, insensate, drills its brutal way
Through quivering hearts and sets men's pulses mad
With burning rage to rend the strong and fair,
If only they were born on other shores.

. . .

And yet – tonight – our young men from the town
Sleep under the high arches of the stars
And keep their watch in crystal, moonlit air,
Perforce within God's presence, too.

FORGOTTEN DEAD, I SALUTE YOU

Dawn has flashed up the startled skies,
Night has gone out beneath the hill
Many sweet times; before our eyes
Dawn makes and unmakes about us still
The magic that we call the rose.
The gentle history of the rain
Has been unfolded, traced and lost
By the sharp finger-tips of frost;
Birds in the hawthorn build again;
The hare makes soft her secret house;
The wind at tourney comes and goes,
Spurring the green, unharnessed boughs;
The moon has waxed fierce and waned dim:
He knew the beauty of all those
Last year, and who remembers him?

Love sometimes walks the waters still,
Laughter throws back her radiant head;
Utterly beauty is not gone,
And wonder is not wholly dead.
The starry, mortal world rolls on;
Between sweet sounds and silences,
With new, strange wines her beakers brim:
He lost his heritage with these
Last year, and who remembers him?

None remember him: he lies
In earth of some strange-sounding place,
Nameless beneath the nameless skies,
The wind his only chant, the rain
The only tears upon his face;
Far and forgotten utterly
By living man. Yet such as he
Have made it possible and sure
For other lives to have, to be;
For men to sleep content, secure.
Lip touches lip and eyes meet eyes

Because his heart beats not again:
His rotting, fruitless body lies
That sons may grow from other men.

He gave, as Christ, the life he had –
The only life desired or known;
The great, sad sacrifice was made
For strangers; this forgotten dead
Went out into the night alone.
There was his body broken for you,
There was his blood divinely shed
That in the earth lie lost and dim.
Eat, drink, and often as you do,
For whom he died, remember him.

Millicent Sutherland

ONE NIGHT

I walked into a moon of gold last night,
Across grey sands she seemed to shine so bright.

Wide, wide the sands until I met the sea,
Cradle of moons, yet searchlights followed me.

I asked the moon if creeping round the Zones
She had seen good, or only poor things' bones.

'Pale faces I have seen, unconscious men
Bereft of struggling horror now and then.

'And sinking ships I see, and floating mines,
And cries I hear, "O God", and choking whines.

'But later when the stars shine on the wave
And give more light, I know the dead die brave.

'Passing so quickly from the things that count,
Count to all mortal thoughts, to find the Fount,

'Where angels pour elixir into bowls,
Drink, not for broken hearts, but thirsty souls.'

'And what on shore?' I asked, 'the great Divide
Where rivers run, and trenches side by side?'

'There,' the moon said, 'the snow was on the ground
And the frost pinched me as I beamed around.

'Red pools of gore, and ghastly shadows lay
In deep dug corners, so I sank away.

'Let misty cloudlets sweep across my face
To hide the earth, and give me heart of grace.

'Sudden the air seemed filled with eager breath
Of great Adventurers, released from death,

'And shaking blood from out their eyes and hair
Shouting for further knowledge here and there.

'I lighted these across the treacherous Path
To reach the garden of Life's aftermath.

'And as they sped in troops the great guns boomed,
With flashes lightning swift, and dark hordes loomed,

'And phantom shapes of patient warrior bands –
Then more snow fell and shrouded all the lands.'

. . .

Now pondering from the moon I turned again,
Over the sands, back to our House of Pain.

British Hospital,
Malo, Dunkirk, France

C.A.L.T.

Y.M.C.A.

Oh Monday night's the night for me!
On happy Mondays, after tea,
We canteen helpers drive to ——
(To name the camp would be too rash,
For Zepps our whereabouts might learn
And bombs come dropping in the urn).

We stand and wait behind the bar:
You've no idea how smart we are
At serving Horlick's, tea and 'pop'
To thirsty Tommies, and our shop
Sells cakes, and chocolate and smokes.
We're up to all the little jokes:
And, asked for 'coffin-nails' by wags,
Produce 'Wild Woodbines', well-loved fags.

Some linger for a friendly chat,
Some call me 'Mother' – Think of that!
And often, at the magic word,
My vision grows a little blurred –
The crowd in khaki disappears,
I see them through a mist of years:
I see them in a thousand prams –
A thousand mothers' little lambs . . .

'One bar nut-milk, two scones and teas?
That's fivepence – no; not money please,
Get tickets near the door – for soap,
For note-paper and envelope
Turn to the left' . . . Ah! Tommy dear,
I often wonder if you hear
Me murmur 'Thank you', as I take
Your tickets for the tea and cake,
And tear them up – or understand
I'd like to shake your grimy hand?

Two simple words are all I say,
I've saved them up for many a day –

Just 'thank you', but they mean a lot!
Accept them, for they're all I've got
To tell my gratitude, they come
Straight from my heart. On Monday, some
Five hundred times I say them o'er,
And wish it were five hundred more!

. . .

And when the Camp is wrapped in sleep,
Ere wearily to bed I creep,
Oh Tommy Atkins! brave and true –
I humbly thank my God for you.

August, 1915

Sara Teasdale

SPRING IN WAR-TIME

I feel the Spring far off, far off,
   The faint far scent of bud and leaf –
Oh how can Spring take heart to come
   To a world in grief,
      Deep grief?

The sun turns north, the days grow long,
   Later the evening star grows bright –
How can the daylight linger on
   For men to fight,
      Still fight?

The grass is waking in the ground,
   Soon it will rise and blow in waves –
How can it have the heart to sway
   Over the graves,
      New graves?

Under the boughs where lovers walked
   The apple-blooms will shed their breath –
But what of all the lovers now
   Parted by death,
      Grey Death?

'THERE WILL COME SOFT RAINS'

There will come soft rains and the smell of the ground,
And swallows calling with their shimmering sound;

And frogs in the pools singing at night,
And wild-plum trees in tremulous white;

Robins will wear their feathery fire
Whistling their whims on a low fence-wire;

And not one will know of the war, not one
Will care at last when it is done.

Not one would mind, neither bird nor tree,
If mankind perished utterly;

And Spring herself, when she woke at dawn,
Would scarcely know that we were gone.

Lesbia Thanet

IN TIME OF WAR

I dreamed (God pity babes at play)
   How I should love past all romance,
And how to him beloved should say,
   As heroes' women say, perchance,
      When the deep drums awake –
      'Go forth: do gloriously for my dear sake.'

But now I render, blind with fear,
   No lover made of dreams, but You,
O You – so commonplace, so dear,
   So knit with all I am or do!
      Now, braver thought I lack:
      Only God bring you back – God bring you back!

Aelfrida Tillyard

INVITATION AU FESTIN

Oh come and live with me, my love,
   And share my war-time dinner.
Who eats the least at this our feast,
   Shall make John Bull the winner.

Here is a plate of cabbage soup,
   With caterpillars in.
How good they taste! (Avoid all waste,
   If you the war would win.)

Now, will you have a minnow, love,
   Or half an inch of eel?
A stickleback, a slice of jack,
   Shall grace our festive meal.

We've no unpatriotic joint,
   No sugar and no bread.
Eat nothing sweet, no rolls, no meat,
   The Food Controller said.

But would you like some sparrow pie,
   To counteract the eel?
A slice of swede is what you need,
   And please don't leave the peel.

But there's dessert for you, my love,
   Some glucose stewed with sloes.
And now good-night – your dreams be bright!
   (Perhaps they will – who knows?)

A LETTER FROM EALING BROADWAY STATION

(From E.M.W.T.)

'Night. Fog. Tall through the murky gloom
The coloured lights of signals loom,
And underneath my boot I feel
The long recumbent lines of steel.

As up and down the beat I tramp
My face and hair are wet with damp;
My hands are cold – that's but a trifle –
And I must mind the sentry's rifle.
'Twould be a foolish way to die,
Mistaken for a German spy!
Hardest of all is just to keep
Open my eyelids drugged with sleep.

Stand back! With loud metallic crash
And lighted windows all a-flash
The train to Bristol past me booms.

I wonder who has got my rooms!
I like to think that Frank is there,
And Willie in the basket-chair,
While Ernest, with his guileless looks,
Is making havoc in my books.
The smoke-rings rise, and we discuss
Friendship, and What Life Means to Us,
What is it that the kitchens lack,
And where we'll take our tramp next vac.

Those girls at Newnham whom I taught
I'll spare them each a friendly thought . . .

An hour to dawn! I'd better keep
Moving, or I shall fall asleep.

I've had before my eyes these days
The fires of Antwerp all ablaze.
(The startled women scream and weep;
Only the dead have time to sleep.)
I'd like to feel that I was helping
To send the German curs a-yelping.
Well, if I serve the Belgian nation
By guarding Ealing Broadway station,
I'll guard it gladly, never fear.

Sister, good-night; the dawn is here.'

Cambridge, October 11, 1914

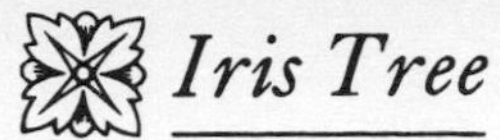

Iris Tree

Poem untitled

Of all who died in silence far away
Where sympathy was busy with other things,
Busy with worlds, inventing how to slay,
Troubled with rights and wrongs and governments and kings.

The little dead who knew so large a love,
Whose lives were sweet unto themselves a shepherding
Of hopes, ambitions, wonders in a drove
Over the hills of time, that now are graves for burying.

Of all the tenderness that flowed to them,
A milky way streaming from out their mother's breast,
Stars were they to her night, and she the stem
From which they flowered – now barren and left unblessed.

Of all the sparkling kisses that they gave
Spangling a secret radiance on adoring hands,
Now stifled in the darkness of a grave
With kiss of loneliness and death's embracing bands.

No more! – And we, the mourners, dare not wear
The black that folds our hearts in secrecy of pain,
But must don purple and bright standards bear,
Vermilion of our honour, a bloody train.

We dare not weep who must be brave in battle –
'Another death – another day – another inch of land –
The dead are cheering and the ghost drums rattle' . . .
The dead are deaf and dumb and cannot understand. . . .

Of all who died in darkness far away
Nothing is left of them but LOVE, who triumphs now,
His arms held crosswise to the budding day,
The passion-red roses clustering his brow.

1917

Iris Tree

Poem untitled

And afterwards, when honour has made good,
And all you think you fight for shall take place,
A late rejoicing to a crippled race;
The bulldog's teeth relax and snap for food,
The eagles fly to their forsaken brood,
Within the ravaged nest. When no disgrace
Shall spread a blush across the haggard face
Of anxious Pride, already flushed with blood.

In victory will you have conquered Hate,
And stuck old Folly with a bayonet
And battered down the hideous prison gate?
Or will the fatted gods be gloried yet,
Glutted with gold and dust and empty state,
The incense of our anguish and our sweat?

1917

Alys Fane Trotter

THE HOSPITAL VISITOR

When yesterday I went to see my friends –
  (Watching their patient faces in a row
I want to give each boy a D.S.O.)
When yesterday I went to see my friends
With cigarettes, and foolish odds and ends,
  (Knowing they understand how well I know
That nothing I can do may make amends,
  But that I must not grieve, or tell them so),
A pale-faced Iniskilling, just eighteen,
  Who'd fought two years; with eyes a little dim
Smiled up and showed me, there behind the screen
  On the humped bandage that replaced a limb,
How someone left him, where the leg had been
  A tiny green glass pig to comfort him.

These are the men who've learned to laugh at pain.
  And if their lips have quivered when they spoke,
They've said brave words, or tried to make a joke.
Said it's not worse than trenches in the rain,
Or pools of water on a chalky plain,
  Or bitter cold from which you stiffly woke,
Or deep wet mud that left you hardly sane,
  Or the tense wait for 'Fritz's master stroke'.
You seldom hear them talk of their 'bad luck',
  And suffering has not spoiled their ready wit.
And oh! you'd hardly doubt their fighting pluck
  When each new operation shows their grit,
Who never brag of blows for England struck,
  But only yearn to 'get about a bit'.

Katharine Tynan

THE BROKEN SOLDIER

The broken soldier sings and whistles day to dark;
  He's but the remnant of a man, maimed and half-blind,
But the soul they could not harm goes singing like the lark,
  Like the incarnate Joy that will not be confined.

The Lady at the Hall has given him a light task,
  He works in the gardens as busy as a bee;
One hand is but a stump and his face a pitted mask;
  The gay soul goes singing like a bird set free.

Whistling and singing like a linnet on wings;
  The others stop to listen, leaning on the spade,
Whole men and comely, they fret at little things.
  The soul of him's singing like a thrush in a glade.

Hither and thither, hopping, like Robin on the grass,
  The soul in the broken man is beautiful and brave;
And while he weeds the pansies and the bright hours pass,
  The bird caught in the cage whistles its joyous stave.

A GIRL'S SONG

The Meuse and Marne have little waves;
  The slender poplars o'er them lean.
One day they will forget the graves
  That give the grass its living green.

Some brown French girl the rose will wear
  That springs above his comely head;
Will twine it in her russet hair,
  Nor wonder why it is so red.

His blood is in the rose's veins,
  His hair is in the yellow corn.
My grief is in the weeping rains
  And in the keening wind forlorn.

Flow softly, softly, Marne and Meuse;
   Tread lightly all ye browsing sheep;
Fall tenderly, O silver dews,
   For here my dear Love lies asleep.

The earth is on his sealèd eyes,
   The beauty marred that was my pride;
Would I were lying where he lies,
   And sleeping sweetly by his side!

The Spring will come by Meuse and Marne,
   The birds be blithesome in the tree.
I heap the stones to make his cairn
   Where many sleep as sound as he.

JOINING THE COLOURS

(West Kents, Dublin, August 1914)

There they go marching all in step so gay!
   Smooth-cheeked and golden, food for shells and guns.
Blithely they go as to a wedding day,
         The mothers' sons.

The drab street stares to see them row on row
   On the high tram-tops, singing like the lark.
Too careless-gay for courage, singing they go
         Into the dark.

With tin whistles, mouth-organs, any noise,
   They pipe the way to glory and the grave;
Foolish and young, the gay and golden boys
         Love cannot save.

High heart! High courage! The poor girls they kissed
   Run with them: they shall kiss no more, alas!
Out of the mist they stepped – into the mist
         Singing they pass.

Viviane Verne

KENSINGTON GARDENS

(1915)

Dappling shadows on the summer grass,
   Vernal rivalry among the trees;
Lovers smiling coyly as they pass,
   Sparrows laughing in the summer breeze.

Children playing by the placid lake,
   Coaxing ducks, with greedy eyes;
Sunlight gilding ripplelets that break
   Where they struggle for a prize.

Jealous dogs that 'do delight'
   In frantic grappling for a stick,
Racing back with 'bark and bite',
   To yield a trophy quite historic.

Lonely ladies dreaming in bath-chairs,
   Old men taking sun baths on the seats,
Nurses softly talking in prim pairs,
   Telling of their soldier lovers' feats.

Medall'd patrols keeping austere guard
   Over radiant rose and ever-greens,
Gold-flecked finery and velvet sward,
   And the quiet garden of dead queens.

      Fleecy clouds in limpid blue,
         Smiling down with tender mien;
      Life seems simple, honest, true,
         In this simple open scene.

      Who would think that vault benign
         God's last area free from vice,
      Initiates the aerial mine,
         With babes below as sacrifice.

      Sitting here on summer morn,
         With the birds and babes at play,
      Who could dream that sky was torn
         Yesternight – with hellish spray.

It is strange that Nature's lurement
   Waits – unclaimed – for our retrievement,
While men war in false endurement
   Deeming this life's great achievement.

Alberta Vickridge

IN A V.A.D. PANTRY

Pots in piles of blue and white,
Old in service, cracked and chipped –
While the bare-armed girls tonight
Rinse and dry, with trivial-lipped
Mirth, and jests, and giggling chatter,
In this maze of curls and clatter
Is there no one sees in you
More than common white and blue?

When the potter trimmed your clay's
Sodden mass to his desire –
Washed you in the viscid glaze
That is clarified by fire –
When he sold your sort in lots,
Reckoning such as common pots –
Did he not at times foresee
Sorrow in your destiny?

Lips of fever, parched for drink
From this vessel seek relief
Ah, so often, that I think
Many a sad Last Supper's grief
Haunts it still – that they who died,
In man's quarrel crucified,
Shed a nimbus strange and pale
Round about this humble Grail.

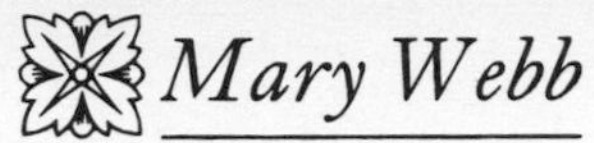

Mary Webb

AUTUMN, 1914

The scarlet-jewelled ashtree sighed – 'He cometh,
For whom no wine is poured and no bee hummeth.'

The huddled bean-sheaves under the moon,
Like black tents, will be vanished soon.
So fast the days draw in and are over,
So early the bees are gone from the clover –
Today, tomorrow –
And nights are dark, and as cold as sorrow.

He's gone, her man, so good with his hands
In the harvest field and the lambing shed.
Straight ran his share in the deep ploughlands –
And now he marches among the dead.

The ash let fall her gems, and moaned – 'He cometh,
And no bee hummeth.'

'O children, come in from your soldier-play
In the black bean tents! The night is falling;
Owls with their shuddering cry are calling;
A dog howls, lonely, far away.'

His son comes in like a ghost through the door.
He'll be ready, maybe, for the next big war.

O world, come in from the leasowes grey
And cold, where swaths of men are lying,
And horror to shuddering horror crying!
Come home
To the wisdom of those that till the loam,
And give man time for his working-day!

Then the white-blossomed ash will sing – 'He cometh,
For whom the loving-cup is poured, the wild bee hummeth.'

M. Winifred Wedgwood

THE V.A.D. SCULLERY-MAID'S SONG

Washing up the dishes;
  Washing up the plates;
Washing up the greasy tins,
  That everybody hates.

Scouring out the buckets;
  Cleaning down the stoves.
Guess I'm going to 'stick it',
  Though my fancy roves.

Washing 'for duration',
  That's what I will do;
As I've got no head-piece
  For the cooking too.

Others are much smarter;
  More clever, too, than I.
Still I go on 'charing';
  Singing cheerfully –

'Washing up the dishes;
  Washing up the plates;
Washing up the greasy tins,
  Which everybody hates.'

CHRISTMAS, 1916

Thoughts in a V.A.D. Hospital Kitchen

There's no Xmas leave for us scullions,
  We've got to keep on with the grind:
Just cooking for Britain's heroes.
  But, bless you! we don't really mind.

We've scores and scores of potatoes,
  And cabbages also to do;
And onions, and turnips, and what not,
  That go in the Irish Stew.

We're baking, and frying, and boiling,
  From morning until night;
But we've got to keep on a bit longer,
  Till Victory comes in sight.

Then there's cutting the thin bread and butter,
  For the men who are very ill;
But we feel we're well rewarded;
  For they've fought old Kaiser Bill.

Yes! we've got to hold on a while longer,
  Till we've beaten the Hun to his knees:
And *then* 'Good-bye' to the kitchen;
  The treacle, the jam, and the cheese!

Catherine Durning Whetham

THE POET AND THE BUTCHER

Milton, thou shouldest be living at this hour,
England hath need of thee. She is a den
Of sugar cards and meatless days and feasts,
Yclept of all their wonted pageantry.
O organ voice of England, who but thee
Could conjure Sunday joints for coupons vile
And fright the butcher from penurious ways,
Provoked by Rhondda and his baleful crew?
Nature, good cateress, once you called her so,
Means her provisions only for the good,
And therefore, looking at the piece of meat
Reposing doleful on our platter blue,
We know we must be bad, O very bad,
And quite unworthy, Milton, John, of you.
That being so, forgive me if I stop
And ask your leave to let the matter drop.

May, 1918

Lucy Whitmell

CHRIST IN FLANDERS

We had forgotten You, or very nearly –
You did not seem to touch us very nearly –
  Of course we thought about You now and then;
Especially in any time of trouble –
We knew that You were good in time of trouble –
  But we are very ordinary men.

And there were always other things to think of –
There's lots of things a man has got to think of –
  His work, his home, his pleasure, and his wife;
And so we only thought of You on Sunday –
Sometimes, perhaps, not even on a Sunday –
  Because there's always lots to fill one's life.

And, all the while, in street or lane or byway –
In country lane, in city street, or byway –
  You walked among us, and we did not see.
Your Feet were bleeding as You walked our pavements –
How *did* we miss Your Footprints on our pavements? –
  Can there be other folk as blind as we?

Now we remember; over here in Flanders –
(It isn't strange to think of You in Flanders) –
  This hideous warfare seems to make things clear.
We never thought about You much in England –
But now that we are far away from England –
  We have no doubts, we know that You are here.

You helped us pass the jest along the trenches –
Where, in cold blood, we waited in the trenches –
  You touched its ribaldry and made it fine.
You stood beside us in our pain and weakness –
We're glad to think You understand our weakness –
  Somehow it seems to help us not to whine.

We think about You kneeling in the Garden –
Ah! God! the agony of that dread Garden –
  We know You prayed for us upon the Cross.

Lucy Whitmell

If anything could make us glad to bear it –
'Twould be the knowledge that You willed to bear it –
  Pain – death – the uttermost of human loss.

Though we forgot You – You will not forget us –
We feel so sure that You will not forget us –
  But stay with us until this dream is past.
And so we ask for courage, strength, and pardon –
Especially, I think, we ask for pardon –
  And that You'll stand beside us to the last.

Margaret Adelaide Wilson

GERVAIS

(Killed at the Dardanelles)

Bees hummed and rooks called hoarsely outside the quiet room
Where by an open window Gervais, the restless boy,
Fretting the while for cricket, read of Patroclos' doom
And flower of youth a-dying by far-off windy Troy.

Do the old tales, half-remembered, come back to haunt him now
Who leaving his glad school-days and putting boyhood by
Joined England's bitter Iliad? Greek beauty on the brow
That frowns with dying wonder up to Hissarlik's sky!

Marjorie Wilson

TO TONY (AGED 3)

(In Memory T.P.C.W.)

Gemmed with white daisies was the great green world
Your restless feet have pressed this long day through –
Come now and let me whisper to your dreams
A little song grown from my love for you.

There was a man once loved green fields like you,
He drew his knowledge from the wild birds' songs;
And he had praise for every beauteous thing,
And he had pity for all piteous wrongs. . . .

A lover of earth's forests – of her hills,
And brother to her sunlight – to her rain –
Man, with a boy's fresh wonder. He was great
With greatness all too simple to explain.

He was a dreamer and a poet, and brave
To face and hold what he alone found true.
He was a comrade of the old – a friend
To every little laughing child like you.

. . .

And when across the peaceful English land,
Unhurt by war, the light is growing dim,
And you remember by your shadowed bed
All those – the brave – you must remember him.

And know it was for you who bear his name
And such as you that all his joy he gave –
His love of quiet fields, his youth, his life,
To win that heritage of peace you have.

Valentine Ackland

7 OCTOBER, 1940

One does not have to worry if we die:
Whoever dies, One does not have to bother
Because inside Her there is still another
And, that one wasted too, She yet replies
'Nothing can tire out Nature – here's another!'
   Fecundity par excellence is here,
   Lying in labour even on the bier.

Maternity's the holiest thing on earth
(No man who's prudent as well as wise
Concerns himself with what is in the skies);
Drain-deep below the slums another birth
   Sets angels singing – the other noise you hear
   May be the Warning, may be the All Clear.

Comfort ye My people! These reflections
Should help them die politely who must die,
And reconcile those left behind, who sigh
For loss of children or some near connections –
   Reflect! There is no need for grief nor gloom,
   Nature has ever another in Her womb.

Teeming and steaming hordes who helter-skelter
Stampede the city streets, to herd together
Angry and scared, in dark, in wintry weather –
Above ground still? Fear not, there's one deep shelter
   Open alike in Free and Fascist State,
   Vast, private, silent and inviolate.

BLACK-OUT

Night comes now
Without the artistry of hesitation, the surprising
Last minute turn-aside into a modulation,
Without the rising
Final assertion of promise before the fall.

Darkness now
Comes by routine of cardboard shutter, rattle of curtain,
Comes like a sentence everyone's learnt to utter,
Undoubted and certain,
Too stupid to interest anyone at all.

NOTES ON LIFE AT HOME, FEBRUARY, 1942

What sounds fetched from far the wind carries tonight,
Do you hear them? Out where the sheep are
Huddled on wintry hill this cold night,
Under the lea of the hill folded;
There on the hard earth the wind goes
Massively over them, burdened with all that has colded
A thousand hearts, emptied a million hearts,
Slain twice and thrice a million. Over it blows
And like a flood pours into the house, under the doors,
Rushing like blood out of the dying veins, over the living it pours
And so, like a cunningly-channelled flood, empties away, departs
Leaving us dirtied with litter of not our own casualties, not our
own hearts.

Mabel Esther Allan

IMMENSITY

You go at night into immensity,
Leaving this green earth, where hawthorn flings
Pale stars on hedgerows, and our serenity
Is twisted into strange shapes; my heart never sings
Now on spring mornings, for you fly at nightfall
From this earth I know
Toward the clear stars, and over all
Those dark seas and waiting towns you go;
And when you come to me
There are fearful dreams in your eyes,
And remoteness. Oh, God! I see
How far away you are,
Who may so soon meet death beneath an alien star.

Late 1940

I SAW A BROKEN TOWN

I saw a broken town beside the grey March sea,
Spray flung in the air and no larks singing,
And houses lurching, twisted, where the chestnut trees
Stand ripped and stark; the fierce wind bringing
The choking dust in clouds along deserted streets,
Shaking the gaping rooms, the jagged, raw-white stone.
Seeking for what in this quiet, stricken town? It beats
About each fallen wall, each beam, leaving no livid, aching place
alone.

March, 1941, after the bombing of Wallasey

Phyllis Shand Allfrey

CUNARD LINER 1940

Now, for the last time, total solitude.
The ship hangs between explosion and quiet forward driving,
The faces of the passengers are grave.
Oh what is this sobriety which so denudes us
Of the sarcastic cough, the cackling laughter,
The thin flirtation and the importance of black coffee after?
Of course, we are all being British, all being ourselves,
All knowing we carry Empire on our shoulders:
But even so, we are exceptionally grave.
Voices: 'My husband's heavily insured.'
'I said to stewardess, get baby into the boat!'
'I carry pneumonia tablets in my old army bag.'

Yes, friends, but if we had no time to scramble
For babies, tablets and insurance papers,
What would the U-boat's dart, the spurting mine
Mean to each one of us? The end of *what*?

The end of helpless dignity for the army officer!
The end of dancing for the golden girl:
The end of suckling babies for the mother:
The end of study for the gangling youth:
The end of profit for the business men:
The end of brave sea-faring for the crew:
But for so many it would be the end of nothing,
Of nothing nicely done and dearly cherished.

And for myself? oh darling, for myself
It would be life's most true and fatal end;
It would be the conclusion in my brain
And my most spirited heart and my fair body
Of you – the last rich consciousness of you.

YOUNG LADY DANCING WITH SOLDIER

Young lady dancing with soldier,
Feeling stern peaty cloth with your slight hand,
So very happy,
So happy
To be dancing with the patriotic male –
You have forgotten
deliberately
(Or perhaps you were never concerned to know)
Last month your partner was a shipping clerk.

How, as he sat by his few inches of window,
This boy dreamed of ships and far engagements,
Battles with purpose
and future,
Fair women without guile, and England's honour,
Comme chevalier
sans peur . . .
But instead he got conscripted into the Army,
And now you are the last symbol of his dream.

It is rather thrilling to be a last symbol,
Before mud clogs the ears, blood frets the mouth
Of the poor clerk
turned soldier,
Whose highest fortune will be to find himself
Conscripted back
to life . . .
Done up like a battered brown paper parcel –
No gentleman, *malgré tout*; clerk unemployed.

Mary Désirée Anderson

HARVEST

In open country the September fields
Now face the death of harvest, and their powers
Through ruthless loss redouble their ability,
But here, the blackened dust of London shields,
With artificial pomp of bedded flowers,
The helpless shame of its outworn sterility.

There death is rich in promised life, but here,
When our bright masqueraders freeze and sicken,
We have no power to give them fresh fertility.
Thus, through the smiling scorn of this dread year,
We stand inert and see our comrades stricken,
Our hands unarmed, ashamed of our futility.

We watch afar and mark the hideous pace
At which the Reaper moves; like corn our pride
Bows its plumed head to dark humility,
Nor have we vision to discern some place
Where, from the furrowed grave of hopes that died,
Point the bright blades of immortality.

THE BLACK-OUT

I never feared the darkness as a child,
For then night's plumy wings that wrapped me round
Seemed gentle, and all earthly sound,
Whether man's movement or the wild,
Small stirrings of the beasts and trees, was kind,
So I was well contented to be blind.

But now the darkness is a time of dread,
Of stumbling, fearful progress, when one thinks,
With angry fear, that those dull amber chinks,
Which tell of life where all things else seem dead,
Are full of menace as a tiger's eyes
That watch our passing, hungry for the prize.

Over all Europe lies this shuddering night.
Sometimes it quivers like a beast of prey,
All tense to spring, or, trembling, turns at bay
Knowing itself too weak for force or flight,
And in all towns men strain their eyes and ears,
Like hunted beasts, for warning of their fears.

Juliette de Bairacli-Levy

KILLED IN ACTION

His chair at the table, empty,
His home clothes hanging in rows forlorn,
His cricket bat and cap, his riding cane,
The new flannel suit he had not worn.
His dogs, restless, restless, with tortured ears
Listening for his swift, light tread upon the path.
And there – his violin! Oh his violin! Hush! hold your tears.

For N.J. de B.-L.
Crete, May, 1941

THRENODE FOR YOUNG SOLDIERS KILLED IN ACTION

For all the young and the very lovely
  Who will come no more to an earthly home,
For all such virgin trees cut by death's axe –
  How can I for such a sacrifice atone?
Could my silver lakes of tears be enough?
  The long threnodes my tinsel nightingales sing?
No not enough! oh not nearly enough!
  I would find a more splendid offering.

For all the talented and the gallant
  Who will tread no more any earthly place,
For unknown painters and poets burnt by death's flames –
  How can I perform sufficient penance?
What of long fastings and a crown of thorns?
  Could prayers and sackcloth ever suffice?
No not enough! oh not nearly enough!
  Only my life would be fair sacrifice.

Joan Barton

FIRST NEWS REEL: SEPTEMBER 1939

It was my war, though it ended
When I was ten: could I know or guess
What the talking really said?
– 'Over the top. At the front.
Sealed-with-a-loving-kiss.
Train-loads of wounded men
At the old seaside station.
Two million dead' –
Child of the nightmare-crying 'Never again'.

The same 'I' sits here now
In this silent throng
Watching with dull surprise
Guns limbering to the line
Through umber sheaves,
Guns topped with dappled boys
And crowned with beckoning leaves,
Like floats for some harvest home
Of corn or wine;

A self removed and null
Doubting the eye that sees
The gun in its green bower,
Yet meticulously records
At each load, discharge, recoil,
How the leaves spin from the trees
In an untimely shower
Over the sunlit fields, and are whirled away
To the edge of the sky.

No mud. No wounds. No tears.
No nightmare cries. Is it possible
It could be different this time?
Far-off that passing bell
Tolls 'Different.
Yes always different. Always the same':
As the guns roar and recoil
And the leaves that spin from the trees
Deck boys for a festival.

Joyce Barton

EPITAPH ON A SOLDIER

In some far field my true-love lies,
His flooded heartblood growing cold;
The mask of death is on his eyes,
His life this day for freedom sold.

Nor will his loss remembered be,
When others desecrate the truth
In later years, except by me –
For with his passing went my youth.

Rachael Bates

THE INFINITE DEBT

A stranger died for me,
   Groaned and dropped and died somewhere –
His fire quenched utterly
   In a shrivelling air.

And how shall I requite
   His wounds, his death, who dies unknown
And keeps my feeble flame alight
   With ransom of his own?

All life, all love's his fee
   Whose perished fire conserves my spark,
Who bought the brightening day for me
   And for himself, the dark.

HOW SWEET THE NIGHT

How sweet, how sweet will be the night
When windows that are black and cold
Kindle anew with fires of gold;

When dusk in quiet shall descend
And darkness come once more a friend;

When wings pursue their proper flight
And bring not terror but delight;

When clouds are innocent again
And hide no storms of deadly rain;

When the round sky is swept of wars
And keeps but gentle moon and stars.

Lord, who doth even now prepare
That peaceful sky, that harmless air –
How sweet, how sweet shall be the night!

Marjorie Battcock

THE REFUGEE

Mud dark above the stream the factory's finger
Points through the rain towards a sodden sky,
Setting and cold crush her desire to linger,
Barred shops and shuttered windows mute the street,
The scene's decay is like an ugly cry.

She turns towards her home, a furnished room,
Its paint beer-brown, its three-piece, saxe-blue plush,
Where a bald light diminishes the gloom,
But leaves her chilled, and turns her thoughts towards,
The foreign city that was once her home, lush

In the summer with grape-green linden trees;
Evenings of music, cafés, interchange
Of differing views; all this she sees,
Vivid in retrospect, each richly-textured day
Ended with war; instead the pinchbeck range

Of work's monotony, that dims her pride
In memories. But for this isolation
She blames herself – friends have been tortured, died,
She, rootless, without future, should be glad,
And being so, deny her desolation.

Vera Bax

TO RICHARD, MY SON

(Killed in Action, August 17, 1942)

I hide my grief throughout the weary days,
And gather up the threads of life again,
Remembering you ever gave your praise
To those for whom fate's hardest thrust was vain.
Now, when I feel my courage flicker low,
Your spirit comes to breathe it into flame,
Until I lift my head, and smiling go,
Whispering softly your beloved name.
And yet to me it seems but yesterday
You were a child, and full of childish fears:
Then I would run to you and soothe away
The loneliness of night, and dry your tears;
But now you are the comforter, and keep,
From out the shadows, watch, lest I should weep.

TO BILLY, MY SON

(Killed in Action, May 15, 1945)

Now comes, indeed, the end of all delight,
The end of forward-looking on life's way,
The end of all desire to pierce the night
For gleam of hope, the end of all things gay;
The end of any promise Spring might hold,
The end of praying and, O God, the end
Of love that waited to be shared and told;
Now, evermore, shall life with sorrow blend;
That sorrow whose dark shape the months had fought,
And strictly kept in confines of the will;
Had held quiescent while each conscious thought
Searched far horizons where joy lingered still;
But, my beloved, fearless, gallant, true,
Here is fair end of sorrow, now, for you.

THE FALLEN

(V.J. Day, August 15, 1945)

Have no self-pity now for loneliness;
Permit no tear, no sad, recalling sigh
For these, the dead, who counted all things less
Than honour, and the courage so to die;
Remembering that age too seldom gives
What youth has dreamed: our hopes are mostly vain
And fortunate indeed is he who lives
Forever young, beyond the reach of pain.
Yours is the sorrow, heart that still must beat,
Yours is the heavy burden of the day,
Yours the long battle now against defeat,
Be not less steadfast in the fight than they;
Nor shun the throng: their spirits linger there,
Whose laughter rang so gaily on the air.

Mary Beadnell

HIROSHIMA

Hi-ro-shi-ma
Hi-ro-shi-ma
Shrine of tinkling bells
and beauty blossoming,
petalled in paper houses
with an artist's landscape,
brush and soft pen . . .
all gold and pale rose-mist
(With bamboo leaves).

Within your heart, delicate,
like a bird's wing,
there is an unborn cry.
I feel it here,
still . . .
a pang within my breast,
this sorrow torn
from the tomb of Science
and derelict destruction.

I can see
that mushroom hanging,
hovering ominously
even on a clear, bright
summer's day –
Amid the clapping voices
of children,
and soft, unspoken words
like silk and sake:
Amid the chatter of rice-tables,
square, low,
and cushions:
Amid the tap of tiny women
in kimonos,
their black hair framing
moon faces and with
large eyes . . .
that do not accuse me.

Audrey Beecham

SONG

There's no more talk and ease
No more time to do as you please
Pressure of men on roads, of boots and heels,
Lorries and guns, and birds again
This winter will freeze.

War comes flooding like a tide
O where shall we run, shall hide?

Setting out or turning back,
The old wound split in new strife,
A new wound is a new eye
A festering wound a womb of different life.

Where shall we hide but in the wound?

DITTY

If this town should tumble down
No one would be sorry.
We'd take to the fields
And have our meals
Of bracken and prickly holly.

If these spires should once be mired
In rubble dust and water
We'd sail like ducks
Past all the clocks
And gaily shop by barter.

If we should lack a cloth to our backs
Huddled in earth together
The life of man
Is quickly spanned
And earth goes on for ever.

EICHMANN

Incense of Belsen is stench in the nostrils of heaven
Ashes of Ravensbruck idly drift over the air
Lightly touch down in the teacups of innocent parties
Dusting with grey the blondest of teenage-dyed hair.

What shall I say to the books and the films and the stories?
That if I was not, I might have been, almost was there
When the German Longinus stood guard at the Jew's crucifixion
And under that same condemnation all men took a share.

The Roman Church celebrates Longinus, the soldier who pierced Christ's side, on March 15th; and the Greek Church celebrates Longinus, the Centurion, on October 16th.

Frances Bellerby

INVALIDED HOME

He is coming back.
The child would retreat only under protest,
But the man will come without protesting.

Will he come to stay?
Here, deeply at-home, he could perhaps rest,
At last content with resting.

Here he could lie,
Listen to the stream, and easily forget
The discipline of forgetting.

Not a single voice
Of the water would be new. He would hear
Conversation he was used to hearing

As a child in bed;
Would understand, mind luminous with dream,
As the child, half-dreaming,

Understood the whole thing.
And would soon, like the drowsy child, accept
All that needs accepting.

. . .

But do you think he will stay
Even as long as the daffodils out there
Under the apple tree –
Brushed tenderly
On the frost-grey grass and the translucent air
This opening day?

WAR CASUALTY IN APRIL

If Man has forgotten tenderness, yet it remains
With the birds feeding the anxious fluttering young.
If Man has rejected compassion, still there persists
As of old the heart-wrenching droop in missel-thrush song.
And Man dreams not of faithfulness such as the lilac tree
Flaunts undismayed beside the broken home.

The brown-coated bulb lay tombed in the drowsing earth
But never forgot its springtime tryst with Life;
Yet Man keeps no tryst with Life: he obliterates
Memory, and hope; he labours to destroy;
Serves Death; cages the iridescent wings,
Gags back the golden song, crucifies love;
Mercy denies.

  Yet the mercy of the grass
Warm sweetness breathes into this dying face,
And the tender charity of the gentle rain
Washes away the blood from these death-clouded eyes.

Elizabeth Berridge

BOMBED CHURCH

The heart of the church is broken
Chancel cracked across and
Gone the fragrant-swinging boys.
Echoes are hymnals
Shadows the congregation.
All over London now the spires
May not aspire, and steeples
Are laid as low as the lowest peoples.
Bats descend and flap
If the rusty verger shuffles back.
Once, he told me. Once, he said
In a whisper,
He heard a black owl chant the lesson.

Marjorie Boulton

SPRING BETRAYED

For a man of seventy-six, going to Egypt to mourn his only son, killed on active service

Time for the brave would be algebra, terminal
trick of the sun, formula, concept of causes,
the propertied moments being unplaced and eternal,
save for death for the female blood and the seasonal forces;
and the screamed Yes of a son bright from the womb
sets free the father from time:
the permanent cycle, the seasons completed,
life with rich counterpoint promised repeated.

But the formulation of seasons cheated
where under the callous recording Egyptian sun
where the grooved sand made of grained bones is heated
the man with lunar hair lost his only son
from the seasonal madness of man and the legend of force,
the tank's inorganic course:
betrayal of time, the pagan oracles dumb,
aged David lamenting for Absalom.

To tricked parent no heir-apparent can come.
The rites of Spring are maimed and the vegetation
withers, the seasonal heartbeat a muffled drum
where minus cancels all meaning from marriage equation,
Egyptian rivers run purple down to the sea,
small gardens wilt in a day;
O son in long sands set, O scholar denied all reasons,
where is a word, a light, to restore the reversal of seasons?

1946

Anne Bulley

LEAVE POEM

O let the days spin out
In leisure, as the clouds pass;
Weave webs of shadow
Across the grass.

Let nothing touch me now,
But the minty mountain air,
Sun, wind and your fingers
Through my hair.

And when the hills grow cold
Outside, lock out the night,
Tell me long tales and stir
The fire bright.

For I would be bastioned here
Against the constant hum
Of streets and men and ships
Whence we have come.

So let the days spin out
In magic hours and laughter
That I may hold the thought
Long, long after.

Christina Chapin

ON A BOMB HEARD THROUGH A VIOLIN CONCERTO

The music rises in a wall of light
Against delirium and the world's dark dream;
Etched on the glory of its upward stream
The naked tree of truth lives in our sight
Rimmed with its radiancy. Our clear midnight
With the clean fragrance of its lifted theme
Is fresh and singing; its triumphant gleam
Grows and distils a vision sharp and bright.

And at the last the heart of us takes wing
Into the heart of peace where beauty lies –
Is kindled with the light that cannot fade.
The silent music still goes echoing
Through the dim vaults where never echo dies;
Knowledge is born and lovely deeds are made.

Sarah Churchill

THE BOMBERS

Whenever I see them ride on high
Gleaming and proud in the morning sky
Or lying awake in bed at night
I hear them pass on their outward flight
I feel the mass of metal and guns
Delicate instruments, deadweight tons
Awkward, slow, bomb racks full
Straining away from the downward pull
Straining away from home and base
And I try to see the pilot's face.
I imagine a boy who's just left school
On whose quick-learnt skill and courage cool
Depend the lives of the men in his crew
And success of the job they have to do.
And something happens to me inside
That is deeper than grief, greater than pride
And though there is nothing I can say
I always look up as they go their way
And care and pray for every one,
And steel my heart to say,
'Thy will be done'.

R.A.F.

We will remember
We promise you
Whatever life may bring,
When river mists creep up and chill
And birds who love the Summer, wing
Their way to kinder skies
Fearing the wild December
We will remember
We promise you.

We will remember
We promise you
If ever life should bring
Some measure to our dearest dream
And once again there should be Spring
And we should live to know
A kindlier December
We will remember
We promise you.

We will remember
We promise you
Whatever may unfold
Be there but bitterness to reap
Still in despair we'll never lightly hold
That which you loved and gave without a thought
How could we cheapen
What was so dearly bought.
In Spring, in Summer and in December
We will remember
We will remember.

Lois Clark

FLASHBACK

I remember waking
from a sort of sleep,
khaki-clad and rigid on the canvas bed,
gas mask already slung
like an obscene shoulder-bag;
torch in one hand, tin hat in the other,
and the blasted buzzer shaking
the waking brain to jelly,
mercilessly dragging the tired body up
out of exhausted oblivion.

First out tonight.
Feet into rubber boots,
stumble down the darkened corridor,
burst through the black-out into the noisy yard
where the cars stand patiently,
their burden of stretchers
outlined against a blazing sky.

Fumble for the lock of the old Ford –
'Put out that bloody torch!'
squeeze in behind the wheel, wait for the men;
three bearers pile in the back
loud with their cockney curses,
the leader beside me
'Now lads, remember there's a lidy in the car'.

Pull the starter, oh God make her go!
She goes. Across the yard,
double declutch at the gate, and out –
roaring down the now invisible road,
masked sidelights only –
roaring down to disaster;
where the bomb-ploughed houses wait
with their harvest of casualties.

PICTURE FROM THE BLITZ

After all these years
I can still close my eyes and see
her sitting there,
in her big armchair,
grotesque under an open sky,
framed by the jagged lines of her broken house.

Sitting there,
a plump homely person,
steel needles still in her work-rough hands;
grey with dust, stiff with shock,
but breathing,
no blood or distorted limbs;
breathing, but stiff with shock,
knitting unravelling on her apron'd knee.

They have taken the stretchers off my car
and I am running
under the pattering flack
over a mangled garden;
treading on something soft
and fighting the rising nausea –
only a far-flung cushion, bleeding feathers.

They lift her gently
out of her great armchair,
tenderly,
under the open sky,
a shock-frozen woman trailing khaki wool.

FLY PAST ALDERNEY

Engines grumble behind the mist.

Lumbering out of limbo into a blue morning,
the Wellington tows its bulky shadow
over sea and cliffs,

its belly empty of bombs,
twin Spitfires
a pair of dogs at heel.

Like a woman who has forgotten rape,
the island dozes, cosy in sunlight;
no echoes shiver her still pools,
no memories play back the tramp
of jackboots
across her mossy breasts.

The harbour wall shelters little ships
with a father's arm;
the emaciated shuffle of slaves,
the whiplash and the wailing
are faded now
into the passing cry of gulls.

And bodies, flung like refuse
into the dark chambers of her soil,
rotted long ago,
forgotten
where now pink thrift spreads
thickly above their bones.

Fortresses crumble on the cliffs
among the ghosts of guns
and concrete bunkers battened down with gorse
only jagged dentures of rock
hold danger now, and currents
hurrying to slap against their sides.

As these few thunderous moments pass
over our heads, only the old
with mainland memories, pollute
this clear channel air with fear,
and drag
out of an interrupted youth
the dim rag dolls of death.

Battle of Britain Day 1977

Alice Coats

SKY-CONSCIOUS

Now we are forced to contemplate the sky,
So long before an unregarded roof –
Now charged with such significance, the proof
Of potencies whereby we live or die;

Frescoed with searchlights, shells and flares and stars,
Trellised with trailing fumes of alien flight,
Lit with false dawn of fires, and all the bright
Ferocious constellations of our wars.

In these we read the portents of our end
And turn in fear to scan the skies again,
For dooms like those the gods were used to send
Whose rule no longer sways their old domain –

Jove's superseded thunderbolts at rest,
Aurora and Apollo dispossessed.

THE 'MONSTROUS REGIMENT'

What hosts of women everywhere I see!
I'm sick to death of them – and they of me.
(The few remaining men are small and pale –
War lends a spurious value to the male.)
Mechanics are supplanted by their mothers;
Aunts take the place of artisans and others;
Wives sell the sago, daughters drive the van,
Even the mansion is without a man!
Females are farming who were frail before,
Matrons attending meetings by the score,
Maidens are minding multiple machines,
And virgins vending station-magazines.
Dames, hoydens, wenches, harridans and hussies
Cram to congestion all the trams and buses;
Misses and grandmas, mistresses and nieces,
Infest bombed buildings, picking up the pieces.

Girls from the South and lassies from the North,
Sisters and sweethearts, bustle back and forth.
The newsboy and the boy who drives the plough:
Postman and milkman – all are ladies now.
Doctors and engineers – yes, even these –
Poets and politicians, all are shes.
(The very beasts that in the meadows browse
Are ewes and mares, heifers and hens and cows. . . .)
All, doubtless, worthy to a high degree;
But oh, how boring! Yes, including me.

Marion Coleman

MONTE CASSINO 1945

The old snow-summitted mountains
stand back in the spring light,
sheltering wide plains.
Here white almond flower shakes on the wind,
pruned vines and figs swell knotty buds,
green corn presses under the olives,
willow canes spring yellow from pollard trunks.
The road steps among fields and villages,
twists round little hills,
runs up and down through high towns
built in dangerous days
when life was hunted by death.

The houses are broken, wasted,
fields and trees wounded, killed.
Crosses crowd where corn grew,
sprouted from bodies hurriedly buried,
sown deep and thick in the raked soil.
Warm air distils
a scent, not of flowers and young leaves,
but of putrid decay,
heavy as magnolia, horribly rotten.
Pools shine among splintered stones,
life remaking in their scum.
Behind fragmented buildings, the grey mountain
leans scored, and split, and shaken.

Where light shone, order and praise sang softly,
years of learning were stored
like honey gold in the comb,
now is only bomb-struck desolation.
Death has leapt upon life,
and the shriek of the encounter
echoes on and on through silence
for ever.

Ellodë Collins

CESSATION OF WAR

Will it cease, and the snow,
Gathering on the muzzles of guns,
Lie undisturbed
While the lights of Europe leap and glow
On the cracking of ice as the pent-up waters flow
Bear back our sons?

Will spring see the cessation,
Pale petals flung under their feet
As they come back,
And the budding hopes of a nation
And the smiles and songs and tears which need no explanation
Fill every street?

Will midnight seem hollow,
Warm, soundless, summery, wingless skies,
And they who flew,
Knowing moonlight as a guide to show
Flat silvered roofs and factory chimneys spread below,
See with new eyes?

Will the great news be shouted
Above the sound of threshing wheat,
Bright leaves like flags,
And burdened orchards golden and red,
From toil and strife to green quiet ways to turn instead
Our eager feet?

Frances Cornford

FROM A LETTER TO AMERICA ON A VISIT TO SUSSEX: SPRING 1942

How simply violent things
Happen, is strange.
How strange it was to see
In the soft Cambridge sky our Squadron's wings,
And hear the huge hum in the familiar grey.
And it was odd today
On Ashdown Forest that will never change,
To find a gunner in the gorse, flung down,
Well-camouflaged (and bored and lion-brown).
A little further by those twisted trees
(As if it rose on humped preposterous seas
Out of a Book of Hours) up a bank
Like a large dragon, purposeful though drunk,
Heavily lolloped, swayed and sunk,
A tank.
All this because manœuvres had begun.
But now, but soon,
At home on any usual afternoon,
High overhead
May come the Erinyes winging.
Or here the boy may lie beside his gun,
His mud-brown tunic gently staining red,
While larks get on with their old job of singing.

SOLDIERS ON THE PLATFORM

Look how these young, bare, bullock faces know,
With a simplicity like drawing breath,
That out of happiness we fall on woe
And in the midst of life we are in death.

See how in staring sameness each one stands,
His laden shoulders, and his scoured hands;
But each behind his wall of flesh and bone
Thinks with this secret he is armed alone.

CASUALTIES

This once protected flesh the War-god uses
Like any gadget of a great machine –
This flesh once pitied where a gnat had been,
And kissed with passion on invisible bruises.

AUTUMN BLITZ

Unshaken world! Another day of light
After the human chaos of the night;
Although a heart in mendless horror grieves,
What calmly yellow, gently falling leaves!

N. K. Cruickshank

SNOWY MORNING, 1940

Margined by dirty snow-heaps, pavements puffed and clean,
Slapping through folds of slush with their galoshèd feet,
They plod to work down the middle of the street,
In the narrow fairway as dark as nicotine.

Heads bowed, they meet with silence or good-humoured curse
A sudden snarl of ice in the quick, bitter breeze.
They march like the unemployed or like refugees
Or as though they follow an invisible hearse.

ENEMY ACTION

It has happened before that death came after breakfast
On a scrubbed working day: again and again
Bolts fell, Siloams crumbled, in the past,
Upon the young, the usual, the plain.

And the one who simply went across the road
To post a letter or to look around
Holds his redeemed breath, struggles from a load
Of smouldering dread. After, with what profound

Wonder, what thankful, what extensive fears,
Standing alone in the bright summer weather,
Examines that mild choice, which now appears
A least hinge swinging, lightly as it were a feather,
The vast door, opening, of some forty years.

Elizabeth Daryush

WAR TRIBUNAL

Prisoner, in whose tired bearing still I read
The martial canons of uprightness, pride,
The quiet rules of your too-sounding creed,
Of soaring grasp that your resolve should guide;
In whose wan visage plainly still appear
Marks of the muses' rarer, subtler writ,
Of law melodious that aloft can bear
The mind imperial that has mastered it;

You rode the wind, who tranquil take your fall.
Checked by the fences of terrestrial fate,
Brought up short suddenly by the blank wall,
Calmly your regal thought you dedicate

To this – that grudgingly dull earth may state:
He died with dignity. This is your all.

Barbara Catherine Edwards

A WARTIME MATERNITY WARD

There was no beauty
In the rubble of the tumbled houses,
There was none
In the fearful faces.

The broken limbs
Had lost their symmetry,
The gaping wounds
Unveiled the naked viscera.

There was no music
In the singing sirens;
Only the beat of fear
And the discord of madness.

The crashing guns
Insulted the flimsy eardrums,
The screaming bombs
Echoed our fears.

I thought beauty
Had gone forever
But I looked in their eyes
And there love lingered,

And music soared again
In living voices
And the sound
Was a newborn cry.

BOMB INCIDENT

Stretcher to stretcher still they came,
Young and old all looked the same –
Grimed and battered
Bleeding and shattered
And who they were it hardly mattered.

Barbara Catherine Edwards

Where shall we put
The dogs and cats
The budgerigar
And the cricket bat?

Remnants of lives and forever lost days,
Families ended, minds that were dazed,
Clutched to the breast
Was all they had left
Of life that had gone and homes that were wrecked.
Where shall we put
The shopping bag
The picture of Grandma
The doll of rag?

Covered with dirt and with soot and with dust –
How to begin to clean them up,
To uncover the faces,
Identify people
When nothing is left of human features.
What shall we say
To the waiting friends?
How shall we know
Such anonymous ends?

And some are so still in the hospital beds
Who is dying and who is dead?
The dead must be moved
To make room for the living
But how tell the children tearfully clinging?
What can we say
As they call to a mother?
Or, dead on a stretcher,
A sister or brother.

Whom shall we blame for the folly of war?
Whom shall we tell these stories for?
Who will believe
The sadness of death,
The terror, the fear, and the emptiness –

What can they know
Of the vacant eyes
The sorrow too deep
In the heart that dies?

Ruth Evans

A ROMAN IN LIBYA

Soft sand under my feet, a whiteness of sun obscuring
Distance piled upon distance, as far as human enduring.
Dust in my heart, and bewildered, I stumble to grasp in my hand
The dream of empire I fight for, and lose in the shifting sand.

I think of my happy fountain, bone of Bernini's bone,
Where the dolphins turn in the spray, and water slides over the stone.
Shadows are old where the church door yields leather against my hand:
This is my dream of empire as I lay my arms down in the sand.

Elaine Feinstein

A QUIET WAR IN LEICESTER

the shelter, the old washhouse
water limed the walls
we only entered once or twice
cold as a cellar we
shivered in the stare
of a bare electric light

and nothing happened:
after the war
ants got in the sandbags
builders came

and yet at night
erotic with the
might-be of disaster
I was carried into
dreaming with delight

Mabel Ferrett

WARTIME REPORT CENTRE: SOLO SCHOOL

Two days there were of colour and of sun
that stitched the grass with light, moss-apple-green,
strengthened sky's blue and purple while, in between,
far up the fells, huge cyclopean walls
climbed white and steep by Thorpe and Grassington,

two days so lavish and so prodigal
with bobbing dipper and the yellow bunting
and air like tawny syrup, intoxicating –
now, in the solo school, behind each call
the mind hears yet the blackbird's madrigal,

and sickens at this mend-and-make-do fun,
aching to break from boredom, to go away,
have done with such spayed work, such lustless play,
such lamp-lit prop-and-cop, back to white weirs
that jet and splash and spirtle in the sun.

They will not come, awash off Finistère;
they cannot come who watch by Tunis Gate.
I have no dear one now for whom I wait.
For strangers who outlast the spearing guns
to return home, I smile and call, 'Misère'.

JOHN DOUGLAS WHITE

(Pilot, posted missing, January 1942)

Remembering you, I remember the horse you rode
down Saw Wells; I remember the heat of the day
– was it always summer? – and the scarlet pimpernels
pricking the stubble, and a boy galloping away.
I wonder, did you remember Barkston when
that terrible radiance burst before your eyes
and the heat forced you back, away from your controls
and drove you earthwards from the spinning skies?

You are not forgotten. I still would like to walk
with you and your wife, remembering pleasant things,
assessing cattle and crops and each field's worth;
but earning your wings put an end to more than talk;
we should have met at family gatherings
and celebrated your son's – and son's son's – birth.

Olivia FitzRoy

FLEET FIGHTER

'Good show!' he said, leaned his head back and laughed.
'They're wizard types!' he said, and held his beer
Steadily, looked at it and gulped it down
Out of its jam-jar, took a cigarette
And blew a neat smoke ring into the air.
'After this morning's prang I've got the twitch;
I thought I'd had it in that teased-out kite.'
His eyes were blue, and older than his face,
His single stripe had known a lonely war
But all his talk and movements showed his age.
His whole life was the air and his machine,
He had no thought but of the latest 'mod',
His jargon was of aircraft or of beer.
'And what will you do afterwards?' I said,
Then saw his puzzled face, and caught my breath.
There was no afterwards for him, but death.

WHEN HE IS FLYING

When I was young I thought that if Death came
He would come suddenly, and with a swift hand kill,
Taking all feeling;
Want, laughter and fear;
Leaving a cold and soulless shell on earth
While the small winged soul
Flew on,
At peace.
I used to think those things when I was young,
But now I know.
I know
Death stands beside me, never very far,
An unseen shadow, just beyond my view
And if I hear an engine throb and fade
Or see a neat formation pass

Or a lone fighter soar, hover and dart,
He takes another step more near
And lays his cold unhurried hand upon my heart.

TOAST

All the way back from the air field
Along the jolting road,
Past the paddy fields
And the mud-covered water-buffalo,
I have been pretending to myself
That I am not thinking about letters.
At the door of Regulating I pause,
It is a creed with me never to look for a letter,
If there is one for me it will find me.
Today, feeling bad-tempered, I defy my creed
But there is no letter.
I walk up to the mess.
Irrationally I can feel hot tears in my eyes.
I concentrate on the thought of toast for tea,
Hot toast and lots of butter,
Even jam.
It is something to look forward to for almost ten minutes.
No one answers when I speak,
They are deep in their letters.
I pour milk into my tea and wait for the toast.
They laugh over their letters, and read excerpts,
From a sister in Australia,
From a friend in hospital,
From a friend in France,
I think hard about the toast.
There is no jam but meat paste
And a soft-looking paw-paw which I don't like.
The toast is as good as I know it will be
I crunch it slowly
And the butter runs on to my fingers

And I try not to listen to Wren shop,
To the details of the friend's illness,
To the delinquencies of the dhobi.
I am a little afraid, for when the toast is finished
There will be nothing to look forward to,
And so it was yesterday
And so it will be tomorrow.

Karen Gershon

HOME

The people have got used to her
they have watched her children grow
and behave as if she were
one of them – how can they know
that every time she leaves her home
she is terrified of them
that as a German Jew she sees
them as potential enemies

Because she knows what has been done
to children who were like her own
she cannot think their future safe
her parents must have felt at home
where none cared what became of them
and as a child she must have played
with people who in later life
would have killed her had she stayed

A JEW'S CALENDAR

13th December 1941
In the third winter of the war
all remaining German Jews
were exiled to the Russian front
for what was called resettlement
my father and my mother went
of that alone I can be sure
to make up the six million whose
murder was anonymous

One told me that my father died
in Riga of a stroke in bed
I cannot know if someone lied
I only know that he is dead
for four years in the first world war
he was a front-line soldier

he thought himself a German Jew
and was nobody's enemy

Some said that my mother was
sent to Auschwitz where she died
it may be true but I believe
the transport meant did not arrive
but paced the Polish countryside
until the wagon loads were dead
they killed Jews in so many ways
I know she cannot be alive

Spring 1945
I climbed some stairs to a bare room
in which the Red Cross lists were spread
naming the German Jews not dead
I could not find my parents' names
so glad was I they could not claim
compensation from me for
the martyrdom they had to bear
that I did not grieve for them

Beatrice R. Gibbs

THE BOMBER

White moon setting and red sun waking,
   White as a searchlight, red as a flame,
Through the dawn wind her hard way making,
   Rhythmless, riddled, the bomber came.

Men who had thought their last flight over,
   All hoping gone, came limping back,
Marvelling, looked on bomb-scarred Dover,
   Buttercup fields and white Down track.

Cottage and ploughland, green lanes weaving,
   Working-folk stopping to stare overhead –
Lovely, most lovely, past all believing
   To eyes of men new-raised from the dead.

Virginia Graham

1939 SOMEWHERE IN ENGLAND

Somewhere there must be music, and great swags of flowers,
leisured meals lasting for hours,
and smooth green lawns and roses.
   Somewhere there must be dogs with velvet noses,
and people lounging in big chairs,
and bees buzzing in the pears.
   So short a while, and yet how long,
how long,
since I was idling golden days away,
shopping a little and going to the play!
   Somewhere the red leaves must be fluttering down,
but I am on my way to Kentish Town
in Mrs Brodie's van,
which has no brakes and rattles like a can.
   Tomorrow I shall go to Wanstead Flats
with bales of straw, or a cargo of tin-hats,
or ninety mattresses to aid
the nether portions of the Fire Brigade.
   Not for me a quiet stroll along the Mall,
I must be off to Woolwich Arsenal
with our Miss West;
and it seems I cannot rest,
there shall be no folding of my feet at all
till I have been to Islington Town Hall
with a buff envelope.
   Some day it is my tenderest dearest hope
to have my hair washed, and I
would love to buy
something – anything so long as I could stop
for a moment and look into the window of a shop.
   Somewhere there must be women reading books,
and talking of chicken-rissoles to their cooks;
but every time I try to read *The Grapes of Wrath*
I am sent forth
on some occupation
apparently immensely vital to the nation.

To my disappointed cook I only say
I shan't need any meals at all today.
Somewhere I know they're singing songs of praise
and going happily to matinées
and home to buttered toast,
but I at my post
shall bravely turn my thoughts from such enjoyment.
Ah for the time when, blest with unemployment,
I lived a life of sweet content –
leisured and smug and opulent!
Fear not, Miss Tatham, I am ready as you see,
to go to Romford Hospital or Lea.
Be not dismayed, I will not stray or roam,
Look how I fly to Brookwood Mental Home!
See with what patriotic speed I go
to Poplar, Ealing, Beckenham and Bow!

IT'S ALL VERY WELL NOW

It's all very well now, but when I'm an old lady
I think I shall be amazed, and even a bit annoyed maybe,
when I look back at these years of ceaseless effort
and consider what I did to keep my country free.

If only I were making munitions, or had joined the Forces,
my grandchildren, I know, would not think I'd fought in vain,
but why on earth I did some of the things I am doing now
will be so terribly tiresome to explain.

How can I convince them that it was to England's good
that I went to Waterloo to meet two goats travelling from
Camberley,
and drove them in a car across to Victoria, where I put them in
another train,
third class, non-smoker of course, to Amberley?

Why, do you suppose, when London was burning,
did I find myself alone with a Church Army lady from Rye,

and why did we do nothing at all except drink port and lemon?
(She had a dish-cover on her head, tied on with a Zingari tie.)

And will my children believe me when I tell them
that I carried a flame within me that no mortal power could dowse,
not even when I was made to take a vanload of corsets and molasses
to confuse already hopelessly confused Admirals at Trinity House?

I must confess I sometimes get a bit confused myself.
Why am I doing this? I ask and wonder – why in Britain's name did I do that?
Did I really imagine it would lead us grimly forward to Victory
to share my smoked-salmon sandwiches with the Home Office cat?

All my little war stories will sound so frivolous.
'The old lady is getting very frail,' they will say – 'very soft in the brain';
But I shall nod my head and say, 'Believe me, my children,
in my young days everybody was automatically quite insane'.

Muriel Grainger

LOVE AMONG THE RUINS OF LONDON

In the desolated alleys near Saint Paul's
Dust still falls,
And by Paternoster Row, the bookman's haunt,
Ruins gaunt
Stand uncovered, as though mourning Fleet Street's pride –
Lost Saint Bride.

But in city wastes are churches once concealed,
Now revealed –
All the squalid blocks that hid their ancient stone
Overthrown –
And the quiet benediction of a sunset fires
Wounded spires.

Pricking up between the paving, shoots of green
Now are seen;
In a sheltered niche a bird finds spartan rest
For her nest –
There is love among the ruins; after strife
There is life.

Joyce Grenfell

MARCH DAY, 1941

Taut as a tent the heavenly dome is blue,
Uncrossed by cloud or tossing twig or 'plane,
A measureless span infinitely new
To fill the eye and soar the heart again.
Deep in the wintered earth the shock is felt:
Glossy sweet aconite has shown her gold
And string straight crocus spears, where late we knelt
To lodge their bulbs, are waiting to unfold.
The ragged rooks like tea-leaves in the sky
Straggle towards the earth with awkward grace;
A robin in a silver birch nearby
Thrusts up his carol through the naked lace.
  I've known this day for thirty years and more;
  It will go on as it has done before.

Mary Hacker

ACHTUNG! ACHTUNG!

I'm war. Remember me?
'Yes, you're asleep,' you say, 'and you kill men,'
Look in my game-bag, fuller than you think.

I kill marriages.
If one dies, one weeps and then heals clean.
(No scar without infection.) That's no good.
I can do better when I really try.
I wear down the good small faiths, enough
For little strains of peace, the near, the known,
But not for the big absence, man-sized silences,
Family pack of dangers, primate lusts
I hang on them.

I kill families.
Cut off the roots, the plant will root no more.
Tossed from thin kindness to thin kindness on
The child grows no more love; will only seek
A pinchbeck eros and a tawdry shock.
I teach the race to dread its unborn freak.
I maim well.

I drink gold.
How kind of you to pour it without stint
Into my sleeping throat. In case I die?
You think I'm god, the one that pours the most
Getting my sanction? Well, perhaps you're right.
Divert it, anyway, from the use of peace;
Keep the gross gaol, starvation and the lout,
The succulent tumour, loving bacillus, the clot
As bright as mine, friends all. I pop their prey
Into my bag.

I am the game that nobody can win.
What's yours is mine, what's mine is still my own.
I'm War. Remember me.

Gladys M. Haines

IN WAR

All night the bombers roared about the sky,
    Horror and death scattered beneath their wings:
    And yet I slept – for in far journeyings
My spirit knew again the meads that lie
Where sunlit Stour and Frome flow softly by,
    Past thickets where the willow-warbler sings –
    Deep lanes of woodbine-sweet rememberings,
Green with long ferns between the hedgebanks high!

So through those nights while ever louder grew
The sonorous voice of war, in peace I lay,
Seeming to breathe the air that first I drew;
Danger a thing unknown and far away:
So did I wake to war-scarred London day,
Remembering Dorset fields grey-washed with dew!

Agnes Grozier Herbertson

LAMENT FOR A CORNISH SOLDIER

Let us remember Treverton in all his youth and glory
When dawn breaks on the furzy hill, when noon knows open
  sun,
When eve creeps down the valley way, a minstrel grey and
  hoary,
Calling the name of Treverton, that proud and gallant one.

Let us remember Treverton in all his youth and flower
When night falls on the whitewashed inn and talk flows warm
  and free,
When a step rings on the cobbled path like a bell in a far tower
And someone says 'There's Treverton', – but it is never he.

Let us remember Treverton in all his youth and daring
When others plough the moorland fields and mind the valley
  sheep;
Let us remember Treverton, gone with a wind's caring,
Who had his morning here-along and elsewhere has his sleep.

Let us remember Treverton in all his youth and laughter
When life calls like a singing bird and the heart wakes like a tree,
When lovers wind the Cornish lanes nor grief a shadow after:
Let us remember Treverton who died that this might be.

Phoebe Hesketh

SPRING IN WARTIME

Yesterday
Stark Winter crossed the fields with death,
And paralysed the stirring trees
With cruel breath.
And Spring was in an iron tower
Upon the hill when snow came down
With silent power,
In secrecy, to bury all
The mounds of shovelled earth by night;
And cover all the wounds of war
In stainless white.
The waiting moon
Stared down upon the captive land,
Upon the dark and troubled sea
That washed the sand with waves of blood
Till Spring arose from bitterness.
Now each grim wood
Is loud with song, and branched with light,
And men grown fearless in the sun
Forget the night.

POST-WAR CHRISTMAS

Lean forward Spring and touch these iron trees
And they will come to life!
Unchain the fettered stream, bring warmth to ease
The wounds of Winter's knife.
Lean forward Spring, and I will learn your art
Which out of love has grown.
(War, my life's Winter took my living heart,
And left a heart of stone.)
And though the bright drops on the holly tree
For ageless Christmas shine,
And though the world was saved through agony,
I faint through mine.

For he whose love once bore my grief away,
And made his joy my own,
Sleeps this cold Christmas in a colder clay,
And I must wake alone.
But if a new design for those who mourn
Is shaped through pain,
O Spring, lean forward with creative hands,
And hew this stone again!

Molly Holden

SEAMAN, 1941

This was not to be expected.

Waves, wind, and tide brought him again
to Barra. Clinging to driftwood many hours
the night before, he had not recognised
the current far off-shore his own nor
known he drifted home. He gave up, anyway,
some time before the smell of land reached out
or dawn outlined the morning gulls.

They found him
on the white sand southward of the ness,
not long enough in the sea to be
disfigured, cheek sideways as in sleep,
old men who had fished with his father
and grandfather and knew him at once,
before they even turned him on his back, by the set
of the dead shoulders, and were shocked.

This was not to be expected.

His mother, with hot eyes, preparing the parlour
for his corpse, would have preferred, she thought,
to have been told by telegram rather
than so to know that convoy, ship, and son
had only been a hundred miles north-west
of home when the torpedoes struck.
She could have gone on thinking that
he'd had no chance; but to die offshore,
in Hebridean tides, as if he'd stayed
a fisherman for life and never gone to war
was not to be expected.

Pamela Holmes

PARTING IN APRIL

(1942)

Now like my tears these April blossoms fall,
Borne on the wind, as fragile as a breath;
These days are not for keeping after all,
And we must make quick compromise with death.

The little death we die on this fair day
Points to that parting of a later spring;
No wonder then the faltering heart can say
Nothing, for fear of this foreshadowing.

Only – remember me, when other loves
And other Aprils crowd this one we knew:
When touched by a green breeze the bright earth moves,
Surprising tears within the heart of you.

MISSING, PRESUMED KILLED

There is no cross to mark
The place he lies,
And no man shared his dark Gethsemane,
Or, witnessing that simple sacrifice,
Brought word to me.

There is no grave for him;
The mourning heart
Knows not the destination of its prayer,
Save that he is anonymous, apart,
Sleeping out there.

But though strict earth may keep
Her secret well,
She cannot claim his immortality;
Safe from that darkness whence he fell,
He comes to me.

Pamela Holmes

WAR BABY

He has not even seen you, he
Who gave you your mortality;
And you, so small, how can you guess
His courage or his loveliness?

Yet in my quiet mind I pray
He passed you on the darkling way –
His death, your birth, so much the same –
And holding you, breathed once your name.

Libby Houston

POST-WAR

In 1943
my father
dropped bombs on the continent

I remember
my mother
talking about bananas
in 1944

when it rained,
creeping alone to the windowsill,
I stared up the hill,
watching, watching,
watching without a blink
for the Mighty Bananas
to stride through the blitz

they came in paper bags
in neighbours' hands
when they came
and took their time
over the coming

and still I don't know
where my father
flying home
took a wrong turning

Ada Jackson

BLESSED EVENT

In labour when
the raid began
she could not run
as others ran.
Now here shall be
no infant's cry,
no navel string
to cut and tie,
she being – by
a bomb well sped –
delivered of
her soul instead.

Diana James

THE MUNITION WORKERS

They sat upon a hill,
They could forget
The dark oppressive roof-tops of the town.
They drank their fill;
The buttercups were wet;
The evening sunlight, webbed and mystical,
Transfused the iron bands that were clamped down
On their bright hair; the fetters of the mill
Became a circlet and a coronet.
The wheels poised and the hammers were laid still.

But now the night is deep,
The caverns burn,
The great machine is grinding in a dream.
They cannot weep,
The coronet is stern,
The fountain of their tears has ceased to gleam:
Somewhere men die; somewhere the waters churn
With flame consumed; somewhere the bullets teem
In this dark night, and wreathe their brows with iron,
With the dread weight of an eternal sleep.

Wrenne Jarman

IT HAPPENED BEFORE

Through a mist an army marches,
That was long ago . . .
Down the hill and through the streets,
Tramping heel to toe;
Khaki swaying wrist to shoulder like a muddy sea,
Buttons bright and bayonets fixed,
Only eyes roam free.

And they whistle, whistle, whistle as they go marching by.
Heigh-ho! sweet youth goes out to die.

The tune is 'Tipperary'
And they match it with their stride,
And each man's thoughts wheel homeward
To mother, children, bride.
Past the fields and o'er the bridge and towards the open sea,
And through the docks and out to France –
Stay the dwindling quay!

The women wave their handkerchiefs and feign a brave good-bye.
Heigh-ho! sweet youth goes out to die.

After, came an army back,
Soul-weary and sore,
Through the streets and up the hill
Whence they came before.
But ghosts are marching in their ranks who should not linger there –
Do not gaze into their faces
For their faces are not fair –

But the flags are flying bravely and the mourners are not nigh.
Heigh-ho! sweet youth went out to die.

The vision fades. . . . But hark, a bugle
Sounding in the square!
Strong young life is cheap again –
Khaki masses there!

They are lithe and gay and eager, and courage is their mail,
And they see the bloody combat
As Arthur saw the Grail.

Dry your tears, you silly girl, it does no good to cry.
Heigh-ho! sweet youth grows tall to die!

THE NEUTRAL

As I was walking in the park
I met a blackbird sleek and dark
Who on a rhododendron bush
Warbled to a missel-thrush.
He preened and sang unbridled, for
He cared no whit about the war.

No thought of rationing or raid
Occurred to mar his serenade,
And politicians were to him,
I knew, superfluous and grim.
He honed his beak for an encore;
He cared no whit about the war.

PLASTIC AIRMAN

His face is smooth as sculptured faces are,
His features fair enough to draw a girl's
Arch backward glance, his disciplined blond curls
Swept from a grafted brow without a scar.

But this young mottled face does not betray,
As other faces do, the moods behind –
If he has secrets, they are locked away:
He looks out at the world from a drawn blind
Screening the man he was. And who was he?
Only the grave eyes know, and do not tell. . . .

Be gentle with him, World, who has forgone
His unique pattern, his identity:
Be tender, lest the frozen mask should melt
Abruptly, and surprise us with its scorn.

THRENODY FOR BERLIN – 1945

Was there no mute to mourn this crumpled city,
No funeral drape, no stern bell left to toll?
Does it pass unattended, without pity,
No requiem said for its delinquent soul?

There where the wind plays through the broken copings
And toppled keystones mark the death of streets,
Her veins lie open to the vulture's droppings:
The blood coagulates, and no heart beats.

Go barehead, even her slaves, in this quenched hour –
No Sodom raked to ash five thousand years
Is deader than this mortuum of power,
Watched, in its final rigor, without tears.

F. Tennyson Jesse

NOTE TO ISOLATIONISTS 1940

With you there are blue seas, safe seas,
Ships that go their ways with tranquil breath.
Here there are black seas, cold seas,
And ships unlit that go down to death.

You have the snug homes, the safe homes,
Men who are safe in work or play.
Here there are broken homes, burnt homes,
But hearts undefeated to meet each day.

We have the common men, the quiet men,
Who'd not change the perils that they run
For the safe place and the safe men –
Ours in the shadow for yours in the sun.

Lotte Kramer

CISSIE

Her name was Cissie
And she mangled sheets,
Her hair was peroxide yellow;
She crooned about love
With a smoker's cough
While the sweat slipped down her belly.
She could tell a tale
Full of sex and ale
As the mangle wheeled her story;
And her laughter roared
As her bosom soared
When she slapped the sheets to glory.
In a war-time pub
Some G.I. pick-up
Cheered the Monday morning queues,
But below her pride
Of the good-time night,
Were a lonely woman's blues.
For once in a while
A black eye would smile
From her puffy face, full of sweat;
And we knew it meant
Her old man had spent
The infrequent night in her bed.
So she rolled and roared,
As she laughed and whored
Till one day she clocked-in no more:
No G.I. or mate
Kept her out so late –
But a Buzz-bomb had struck her door.

SCROLLS

If in two thousand years a stumbling boy
Picks up some scrolls in Poland's fleshless plains;
And if efficiency failed to destroy
One charcoaled vest and skirt with needled names;
A handbag with a bracelet or a purse,
A private letter laced with someone's blood;
A picture of a child, some scraps of verse –
All these embalmed in sarcophagal mud:
Someone will write a book of dredged-up tears,
Clutter with sores an exhibition room;
Queues of bright people will poach hunch-backed fears
Chasing the boredom from their Sunday gloom:

Then useless rebels burn as victims fall
Blazing moon-deserts from their wailing-wall.

Carla Lanyon Lanyon

CRUSADE IN EUROPE

Carp and trout, roach and grayling
Uncatchable under the moat bridge
Of an empty Normandy château;
A tethered cow in a field without railing,
Square farm in a square of trees on a ridge
At the edge of the poppied plateau –

Over this open landscape went the tanks,
All those Americans in their white starred trucks
From Oregon and Tennessee;
Into this quiet country broke the Yanks
With ambulances, jeeps and ducks,
Crusading for the name of Liberty.

They came and went away. The same carp lies
Uncaught under the bridge; even the farm still stands
Set in its sea-windbreaker square of trees;
The milch cow with the melancholy eyes,
The crimson clover strip, the barley lands
Resume their mild and several purposes.

But somewhere in Wisconsin in the fall
Eating under a sumac, a hired man
Remembers that those scented fields were warm
In June in France; thinks about his pal
Who came home in a coffin as crusaders easily can,
And the immemorial peasant girl at the farm.

Freda Laughton

THE EVACUEES

There is no sound of guns here, nor echo of guns.
The spasm of bombs has dissolved
Into the determination of the tractor.

Our music now is the rasp of the corncrake
And the wedge-shaped call of the cuckoo
Above leaves tranced in the lap of summer.

We have discovered the grass, curled in the ditches.
We have combed it with rakes in the hayfields,
And coiffed it in lion-coloured stacks.

We have stroked milk, warm and gentle from the cow,
The placid primitive milk, before bottles
Sterilise its mild wonder.

We have met the bland smile of eggs in a willow-basket;
Returned the stolid stare of cheeses ripening on the shelf;
Warmed ourselves at the smell of baking bread.

We have seen food, the sacrament of life,
Not emasculate and defunct upon dishes, but alive,
Springing from the earth after the discipline of the plough.

Margery Lawrence

GARDEN IN THE SKY

There is a monstrous garden in the sky
Nightly they sow it fresh. Nightly it springs,
Luridly splendid, towards the moon on high.
Red-poppy flares, and fire-bombs rosy-bright
Shell-bursts like hellborn sunflowers, gold and white
Lilies, long-stemmed, that search the heavens' height. . . .
They tend it well, these gardeners on wings!

How rich these blossoms, hideously fair
Sprawling above the shuddering citadel
As though ablaze with laughter! Lord, how long
Must we behold them flower, ruthless, strong
Soaring like weeds the stricken worlds among
Triumphant, gay, these dreadful blooms of hell?

O give us back the garden that we knew
Silent and cool, where silver daisies lie,
The lovely stars! O garden purple-blue
Where Mary trailed her skirts amidst the dew
Of ageless planets, hand-in-hand with You
And Sleep and Peace walked with Eternity. . . .

But here I sit, and watch the night roll by.
There is a monstrous garden in the sky!

Written during an air-raid. London, midnight, October 1941

Margery Lea

BOMB STORY (MANCHESTER, 1942)

For a year we lived like troglodytes,
Then a landmine, a near miss,
Blew in the cellar-door.
It flattened my mother's camp-bed.
She rolled under the next one
Murmured, 'How noisy',
And slept peacefully on.

The rectangle of the skeleton doorway
Framed a crimson furnace – the city on fire,
Under the lowering weight of an endless heavy roar
Of the bombers circling – 'theirs', of course;
And over that the booming racket of the ack-ack guns –
'Ours', thank heaven!

Our neighbour descended two floors in her bed
Unhurt; two others were buried.
Another, away for the night,
Rushed home and found it a steaming ruin.
Her mother's Chippendale sideboard –
A few charred fragments – was what
Caused her abandon to helpless tears.

Our windows were all shattered, every one;
The curtains shredded into long vertical strips,
Like the tattered colour of the regiment
After honourable battle.
Our neighbour's garden had a crater that would hold two buses.
He said the rich soil thrown up was most productive,
And round the perimeter he grew excellent lettuces
The next spring of the war.
Meanwhile his wife's lace corselet and her mended red jumper
Hung forty feet up in an elm
Whose leaves were scorched off.

Next morning a Pompeiian pall of dust and smoke
Loomed over all, with hosepipes snaking
Slimily in black mud across the thoroughfares.

One errant spray
Trespassing into our too, too-open windows
Unkindly moistened our National bread and marge,
Our ersatz coffee, and soya-porridge
And straw-pale tea.

But everywhere you could hear the cheerful tinkling
Of broken glass, as housewives swept it up
Into neat heaps on their garden paths;
One bemoaning her Persian carpet's ruin;
Another the grit on her drawing-room settee.
But at seven sharp the milk was on the step,
And at seven-thirty the newsboy came cycling,
Zigzagging among the firemen;
Whistling, surprisingly, an air from a Nocturne of Chopin –
The most beautiful sound in the world.

Patricia Ledward

AIR-RAID CASUALTIES: ASHRIDGE HOSPITAL

On Sundays friends arrive with kindly words
To peer at those whom war has crushed;
They bring the roar of health into these hushed
And solemn wards –
The summer wind blows through the doors and cools
The sweating forehead; it revives
Memories of other lives
Spent lying in the fields, or by sea-pools;
And ears that can discern
Only the whistling of a bomb it soothes
With tales of water splashing into smooth
Deep rivers fringed with ferns.
Nurses with level eyes, and chaste
In long starched dresses, move
Amongst the maimed, giving love
To strengthen bodies gone to waste.
The convalescents have been wheeled outside,
The sunshine strikes their cheeks and idle fingers,
Bringing to each a sensuous languor
And sentimental sorrow for the dead.

Over the human scene stands the old castle, its stone
Now tender in the sun; even the gargoyles seem to find
Some humour in the vision of mankind
Lying relaxed and helplessly alone.
Only the Tudor Roses view with grief
The passing of a kingly age,
The dwindling of a history page,
False-faced religion, sham belief.

Six – the clock chimes for the visitors to go:
The widow reading to her son shuts up the book,
The lover takes his final look
At the mutilated face, so bravely gay;
The young wife, with husband full of shot,
Kisses his brow and quickly walks away,
Her eyes on the stalwart boughs that sway

Still seeing the flatness of his sheets;
The child with dark curls, beloved of all the others,
Jingles his coins and waves bare feet,
Like lily petals, to entreat
One penny more from his departing brother.

One by one the wards empty, happiness goes,
The hospital routine, the usual work
Return for another week;
The patients turn upon themselves, a hundred foes
Imagined swell their suffering;
Fretfully hands pick at sheets
And voices meet
Discussing symptoms and the chance of living.
Only the soldier lies remote and resolutely sane,
Remembering how, a boy, he dreamt of folk
With footballs. Maturity dispelled the dream – he woke
To know that he would never walk again.

EVENING IN CAMP

Mist and cold descend from the hills of Wales,
Relentless as a flood they cover
Deep valley, wood and town,
They creep into our hut,
We cough and shiver:
The oak leaves fall against the door
And somebody murmurs: 'It feels like snow.'
The work is done, the violence of the day
Goes westward with the sun:
To weary senses all things are
The tone of khaki, hair and eyes and skin,
And girls relaxed on chairs and floor are still
With the stillness of saints;
The light is dim and voices
So slow it seems they dream.

At this hour of quietness we wonder:
Where are we? What are we doing?
Perhaps we are players in a Russian scene,
Crouching around the stove discussing
Love and death and the dusty path of time:
Or it may be that we pause
In one of life's vacant places
Where nothing happens,
Where we wait for evolution wondering
What are we doing?

Somebody pokes the fire; the sparks
Rush up the old tin chimney, the coal
Scatters in blue and crimson light.
We remember the pit lads who we saw
Going for lunch through country lanes
To poor cramped homes,
This jet of flame is like the laughter
On their grimy faces.

Some of us think – our thoughts are soft
Because our life is harsh;
Some of us scan the tender, drifting faces
Of our friends to stanch our fear;
We are all so much the same, it is only the weak
Who believe they are different,
Who give themselves airs;
Peace has elusive qualities we do not understand,
We do not turn our minds in that direction,
Nor do we seek for joys not worth the seeking,
But sometimes features shrivel with a lonely pain,
Calling for help we cannot give.

Rest, rest, do not speak. It is right
That the dying year should fill you with dark grief,
Give yourself up to the coming and going of life
Let the leaves and the snow drift over your heart
If you would rise to the sun like a phoenix.

Eiluned Lewis

THE CHILDREN'S PARTY

Quick as shuttles the children move
    Through the lighted room,
Where flowers glow in the scented air
    And candles bloom;
Their voices are fresh as a field of larks
    Over springing wheat;
They weave the web of what is to come
    With their dancing feet.

Like eager ponies snuffing the grass
    And the south-west weather,
Tossing their heads and lifting their feet
    They run together.
By the purring fire on his nurse's knee
    The youngest one
Stretches his toes and his tiny hands
    To catch the fun.

Out in the night, over the snow,
Grimly the dark gun-carriages go,
    Where are they bound for?
        No one knows,
But the curtain shakes,
        Oh, draw it close!

Sylvia Lynd

MIGRANTS

Flecking the sun like autumn leaves,
Today the martins fill the air.
And the round nest beneath the eaves
Will silent be until next year.

But under hot Egyptian skies,
Some English soldier, far from home,
Will watch their flight and hear their cries,
And know that winter's cool has come.

THE SEARCHLIGHTS

All night the searchlights build their towers
With beams and scaffoldings of light;
Or float their water-lily flowers
On the cloud rivers of the dark;
Or weave the sky into a single tent;
Or, like a Harlequin's wand,
Bend an apocalyptic arc
Seeking beyond the reach of sight, –
Beyond it and beyond.
Till, presto! And a transformation scene!
A grey stone forest where dark night has been!
A forest made of stone!
As if all living trees were dead
And pale marmoreal branches raised instead;
But now a slow tide sways the firmament,
And earth beneath her floating weeds lies drowned.
A mad, mad world where all things are
To prettiness and favour turned:
The searchlights that enhance the night,
Bright as the crescent moon is bright,
Cut spear shafts for the moon –
Most lovely when the summer sky
Is like a jewel-box of blue *émail*

Inset with diamond fillet, diamond star;
Encircled by an ash-tree's jet-black frond –
The whole re-echoed in a small round pond.

Lilian Bowes Lyon

A SON

A middle-aged farm-labourer lived here,
And loved his wife; paid rent to hard eternity
Six barren years, till thorn-tree-blessed she bore
A son with a bird's glint, and wheat-straw hair.
  Sweet life! Yet neither boasted.
The boy was a tassel flown by gaunt serenity,
Hedge banner in the September of the War.

A jettisoned bomb fell; at noonday there,
Where take my dusty oath a cottage stood.
Great with unspendable centuries of maternity,
'At least he had struck seven,' she said, 'this year –'
Of different grace; of blood.
The man looks bent; yet neither girds at God,
Remembering it was beautiful while it lasted.

Prudence Macdonald

SPRING 1940

Last spring carried love's garlands – this season a wreath;
broken branches of blossom to decorate death,
cloaking new graves, hardly-won though unsought for,
stainless and free as the causes they fought for.
Yet, begotten of sunlight and suckled by rain,
flowers declare that as surely shall peace follow pain.

AFTER ALAMEIN

You joked, and now are silent; down the years
your wit shall be remembered and revived.
For this blind instant suffer us our tears –
you always drew our laughter while you lived.

Ethel Mannin

SONG OF THE BOMBER

I am purely evil;
Hear the thrum
Of my evil engine;
Evilly I come.

The stars are thick as flowers
In the meadows of July;
A fine night for murder
Winging through the sky.

Bombs shall be the bounty
Of the lovely night;
Death the desecration
Of the fields of light.

I am purely evil,
Come to destroy
Beauty and goodness,
Tenderness and joy.

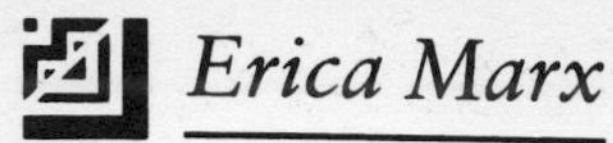

Erica Marx

NO NEED FOR NUREMBERG

From a man to his torturer

You will never forget the look on my face
While you live. As you die
You will see the blue stare of one buried eye
And the spread of my mouth –
No longer a speaking slit in its place
But a buckled distortion, gaping from north to south.

You will never forget: remember the words I can't spill –
You will never forget
How the need of your joy-sick lips for violet
Was deprived of its grin
As your whip came down white in its will
To colour a man undyeable for lack of sinew and skin.

You will never forget what has never been said:
How your torture-bent touch
Found nothing to prey with in a man's crutch –
How your planetless face
Absorbed jellies of blood that obscured a man's head –
Unknowing of reason and language and meaning and Grace.

You will never forget: my mutilate visage will rear
A living and dying reflection of hell and of fear.
It is you by your act who are murdered in light of good sun:
You are cloven, divided, dispersed – you can never be one.

TO ONE PUT TO DEATH IN A GAS CHAMBER

I cannot know how you felt.
I only know
That I might feel the way you felt
When the knock came, and the door
Seeming hard to sound but soft
And easy to the turn of handle
Opened from a slit which widened

In a flash,
While simultaneously a handle turned within yourself,
Like the draw of surgeon's knife
Betrays to air your life's lights –
Secret hidden things.

I cannot know how you felt,
Whether you curried favour, or whether you were great;
Whether against the concrete chimney's light
You shrank, a cowering shade,
Or tall,
Your multiplied-by-indignation soul
Holding the abusers back,
Knew in an ecstasy how to die.

No one will know (head beat against the wall)
How your regrets for living left undone,
So half-toned in their unrelief
To me are perfect in themselves,
And how the whole,
Whether it be complete or unachieved,
Is there, has been, and will be,
Sprawled across this little, living world
In someone's memory.
Your martyred yet unsaintly going
Has its place.

Frances Mayo

LAMENT

We knelt on the rocks by the dark green pools
The sailor boy and I,
And we dabbled our hands in the weed-veined water
Under a primrose sky.
And we laughed together to hide the sorrow
Of words we left unsaid;
Then he went back to his dirty minesweeper
And I to a lonely bed.
O the anguish of tears unshed.

And never again on this earth shall we meet,
The sailor boy and I,
And never again shall I see his face
Framed in a primrose sky,
For the sea has taken his laughter and loving
And buried him dark and deep
And another lad sleeps on the dirty minesweeper
A sleep that I cannot sleep.
O that I could forget and weep.

Naomi Mitchison

THE FARM WOMAN: 1942

Why the blue bruises high up on your thigh,
On your right breast and both knees?
Did you get them in the hay in a sweet smother of cries,
Did he tease you and at last please,
With all he had to show?
Oh no, oh no,
Said the farm woman:
But I bruise easy.

Why the scratched hand, was it too sharp a grip,
Buckle or badge or maybe nail,
From one coming quick from camp or ship,
Kissing as hard as hail
That pits deep the soft snow?
Oh no, oh no,
Said the farm woman:
But I bruise easy.

There was nothing, my sorrow, nothing that need be hidden,
But the heavy dung fork slipped in my hand,
I fell against the half-filled cart at the midden;
We were going out to the land.
Nobody had to know.
And so, and so,
Said the farm woman:
For I bruise easy.

The tractor is ill to start, a great heaving and jerking,
The gear lever jars through palm and bone,
But I saw in a film the Russian women working
On the land they had made their own,
And so, and so,
Said the farm woman:
And I bruise easy.

Never tell the men, they will only laugh and say
What use would a woman be!
But I read the war news through, every day;

It means my honour to me,
Making the crops to grow.
And so, and so,
Said the farm woman:
But I bruise easy.

1943

Bronzer than leaf green, see, the abrupt plover
Expands to a black bright, white flapping flower.
Tumultuous dice-board bird, tumbling, mad in Spring,
Bounced up from earth, down from clouds, to all winds crier,
Furl your self, flower, become bronze, stealthy, crested,
Watcher from pastures. Oh, watch a little, plover,
Nor be too glad this Spring.

May Morton

TO A BARRAGE BALLOON

We used to say 'If pigs could fly!'
          And now they do.
I saw one sailing in the sky
Some thousand feet above his sty,
          A fat one, too!
I scarcely could believe my eyes,
So just imagine my surprise
To see so corpulent a pig
Inconsequently dance a jig
          Upon a cloud.
And, when elated by the show
I clapped my hands and called 'Bravo!'
          He turned and bowed.
Then, all at once, he seemed to flop
And dived behind a chimney-top
          Out of my sight.
'He's down' thought I; but not at all,
'Twas only pride that had the fall:
          To my delight
He rose, quite gay and debonair,
Resolved to go on dancing there
          Both day and night.

          So pigs can fly,
          They really do,
This chap, though anchored in the slime,
Could reach an altitude sublime –
          A pig, 'tis true!
          I wish I knew
Just how not only pigs but men
Might rise to nobler heights again
          Right in the blue
          And start anew!

Margaret Hamilton Noël-Paton

WAR WIDOW

I have grown old and dull, and out of date.
The children – but they are not children now –
They have run on so fast that I am tired,
Left, like a runner who could not stay the course,
Lagging behind.

They don't remember you: they think they do.
They were too young to know you never shared
Their baby world: that your keen, questing mind
Had other fields to travel.

You are not old and dull and out of date!
You are the spare young soldier who looks down
From the tall picture, painted that last leave.
They look at you, and shrug, and their eyes say:
'He would have understood!'

I wonder . . . would you?

Had we grown old together,
I might have slid more gently into age;
You would have altered: touched by autumn's frost
To a more sober russet. As it is, you live
In the shrill green of youth, forever young,
As I last saw you – fifteen years today –
When you went back . . . to that:
And spring-time fled away.

Evangeline Paterson

HISTORY TEACHER IN THE WARSAW GHETTO RISING

The schoolmaster once known as
Umbrella Feet
unfolds his six foot length
of gangling bone

and, mild as usual,
blinks – his bi-focals
having gone the way of his pipe
and his tree-shaded study
and his wife Charlotte –

jacket flapping, as usual,
carpet slippers treading
rubble of smashed cellars,

holding his rifle uncertainly
as if he thought it irrelevant
– as indeed it is –

advances steadily into the
glare of the burning street

leading his scattered handful
of scarecrow twelve-year-olds

towards the last ten minutes
of their own brief history.

FEMALE WAR CRIMINAL

First we are shown the camp. What a precision
of ordered barracks, what a source of pride –
the upper and the nether millstones turning
to grind our death by night and day. And you, mill-girl,
turned them.

Did you wear an overall, mill-girl? Did you keep
your hands clean?

And then your victims, ranged behind the wire,
standing, looking through the camera's eye
to a world they knew no longer how to speak to.
When you see them now, mill-girl,
do you wish they had shouted, or wept?

Or do you remember, mostly,
putting your feet up when your shift was over?

Now, half a lifetime later, you, in daylight,
sharp-eyed with cunning and despair. Knowing
at last which mills grind surest, what do you hope for?

God has more mercy than even you can need,
but you, with your heart shrunk to a small stone
by shutting mercy out, what would you do
with mercy now?

Would you know, mill-girl,
how to receive it, now?

POEM FOR PUTZI HANFSTAENGEL

(Putzi Hanfstaengel was a Nazi and a close friend of Hitler. A man of great charm and culture, he was used to impress foreign visitors. He would also play the piano when Hitler wanted to relax. He finally turned against Hitler, who planned to get rid of him, but he charmed his way to freedom and escaped to America. He appeared on T.V. in the 70s, playing the piano and talking of his friendship with Hitler.)

Doodling on the margin
of history's pages,
playing the piano for your
very good friend,
clever man, fun man,
nice-to-have-around man,
  Oh Putzi Hanfstaengel,
  play for us again!

The ride you went along for
ended on the rapids.
You bobbed like a cork and
you floated again.
Now, on the telly-screen,
soft-spoken, charming,
  Oh Putzi Hanfstaengel,
  play for us again!

Play it for us, like you
played it for Hitler,
and when it's time to go, boy,
you'd better play it then!
Outside the door six
million ghosts are waiting.
  Oh Putzi Hanfstaengel,
  clever Putzi Hanfstaengel,
  fun Putzi Hanfstaengel,
  better swing it then!

Edith Pickthall

EVACUEE

The slum had been his home since he was born;
And then war came, and he was rudely torn
From all he'd ever known; and with his case
Of mean necessities, brought to a place
Of silences and space; just boom of sea
And sough of wind; small wonder then that he
Crept out one night to seek his sordid slum,
And thought to find his way. By dawn he'd come
A few short miles; and cattle in their herds
Gazed limpidly as he trudged by, and birds
Just stirring in first light, awoke to hear
His lonely sobbing, born of abject fear
Of sea and hills and sky; of silent night
Unbroken by the sound of shout and fight.

Cecily Pile

WITH THE GUERILLAS

('All day they hid in the woods' – B.B.C. programme on the Japanese invasion of China)

All day we hid in the woods by the river;
At night, when there was no moon, we ventured into the village.
Food was scarce. It was the sixth year of war.

We have mined the road ahead of a Japanese convoy.
I lie on my back and wait.
The birds in the alder bushes are whistling gaily.

When I was young I lived in a palace with paper windows;
Now I am growing old I have no shelter.
My sons and my daughter's husband were killed in the fighting.

If I were at home again, and the enemy gone from our land,
I could be teaching my little grandson the precepts of virtuous behaviour.

1943

ALL CLEAR

Forget the parallel.
This is quite different – a sweep of sky
Unseen by any living eye,
Here where the green takes hold again
In cities, under rain.
The soft wet different shades of grey
Succour the heart, smooth out the way,
Comfort by sight and smell.
It lifts – it lifts, look up for proof
And see the day break fine,
And all along the crumpled roof
A splinter-shine.

1944

Ruth Pitter

TO A LADY, IN A WARTIME QUEUE

Fourteen months old, she said you were;
And half an hour in bitter cold –
In freezing slush we waited there –
Is surely very hard to bear,
At but one year and two months old.

Your tea-rose cheek grew chill and pale,
The black silk lashes hid your eye:
I thought 'She cannot choose but wail';
I erred, for you were not so frail.
You were determined not to cry.

I saw the lifelong war begin,
One mortal struggle rage, and pass.
I saw the garrison within
Man the frail citadel, and win
One battle at the least, my lass.

You rose to conquer. In command,
Your warrior spirit struck its blow,
Young as the hyacinth in your hand.
No, younger; for I understand
A good one takes three years to grow.

VICTORY BONFIRE

It is a legend already: a wide wide stubble,
Barley-stubble, a hundred pale acres,
With a mountain of straw stacked in the middle, towering,
  looming,
Big as a small hotel. They had ploughed round it
Thirty furrows for a firebreak,
Right away from the house, outbuildings, stackyard,
Right away from the coppice, orchard, hedges:
And high-climbing boys had planted an image of Hitler
On the lonely summit, Adolf forlornly leering.

We made ourselves nests of straw on the edge of the stubble,
In a sweet September twilight, a full moon rising
Far out on the blond landscape, as if at sea,
And the mighty berg of straw was massive before us;
Barley-straw, full of weed-seeds, fit only for burning;
House and barn and low buildings little and hull-down yonder.
People were wandering in, the children noisy, a rumour of
fireworks
Rife among them; the infants never had seen any.
We sat attentive. In their straw nests, the smallest
Piled themselves lovingly on each other. Now the farmer's four
young ones
Stalked over the ploughed strip, solemn with purpose.

Wisps of smoke at the four corners –
Tongues of flame on the still blue evening,
And she's away! . . . A pause, a crackle, a roar!
Sheets of orange flame in a matter of seconds –
And in a matter of minutes – hypnotised minutes –
Vast caverns of embers, volcanoes gushing and blushing,
Whitening wafts on cliffs and valleys of hell,
Quivering cardinal-coloured glens and highlands,
Great masses panting, pulsating, lunglike and scarlet,
Fireballs, globes of pure incandescence
Soaring up like balloons, formal and dreadful,
Threatening the very heavens. The moon climbing
Shakes like a jelly through heated air – it's Hitler!
Look, look! Hitler's ghost! Cheering and screaming –
Some not quite sure how they like it. Now Daddy Foster
Springs a surprise – he's touched off some rockets. O murder!
Knife-edged shrieks from half the young entry!
Buzz-saw howls from the wartime vintage,
For a rocket can only be a V2,
A firecracker a thermite bomb. O hang Daddy Foster!
(So mighty in energy, mighty in influence,
Able to get unobtainable fireworks through Business Contacts.)
There are mothers retreating, taking their weepers with them.
With jangled nerves they execrate Daddy Foster,

Giving him little glory of Business Contacts,
And wondering how long it will be before their infants
Are quiet in their beds. And fireworks will be a lot cheaper
Before they or theirs will squander a sixpence on them.
Little girls from the farm bring lapfuls of apples
From the orchard yonder, picked in the moonlight.
They know the kinds by the shape of the trunks,
So often they've climbed there. These are the earlies,
Worcester Pearmain and Miller's Seedling,
Hard and red in one skirt, soft, milky-pale in the other.
There are drinks, sandwiches, ice-cream out of the baskets,
The glow of the gleed on our faces, and elsewhere
Autumn chill creeping. Into the straw we burrow,
Murmuring and calling, getting colder and sleepier,
And the awns of the barley are working into our souls –
(*Troppo mustachio*, says the Eyetye prisoner)
And the fire is falling, and high and haughty the moon
Shows us our homeward path. Good-nights, then silence:
And the mole-cricket clinks alone, and the stubbles are vacant,
Only blushing and whitening embers left fading and falling.

Nancy Price

TAKE A GUN

Johnny, take a gun – take a gun – take a gun,
Killing's to be done – to be done – to be done,
Never want to run – want to run – want to run,
Finish with your fun – with your fun – with your fun.

Handle steel, – love the feel – death you'll deal,
Pity, mercy crush.
Remember they are mush.
Thousands dead,
Keep your head.
Then you may
Besides your pay
Have a medal pinned –
Hooray!

Ida Procter

THE ONE

In the mass is the one.
In the thousand drowned,
In the hundred shot,
In the five crashed,
Is the one.
Over the news
Falls the shadow
Of the one.

We cannot weep
At tragedy for millions
But for one.
In the mind
For the mind's life
The one lives on.

Sylvia Read

FOR THE WAR-CHILDREN

Out of the fire they come, headlong from heart's desire,
The children, leaping and laughing, and breaking from the
womb;
Bursting aside the foliage of flesh, as through a bush
Plunges a swift racer, or tumbles the wind's rush.

From the white world of the spirit, from the patter of light on
leaves,
The spiralling fall of motes, the gold discs in the ether,
They come, they are born to us. They lie on the sunflaked grass
Cradled in fiery green. They kick, they scatter a mass

Of laughter and leaping fury, the trust of bud, the push
Of light like a hand carrying a candle, a hand with a torch,
Daring its way out of night, from the worm's earth, from under
Thought and dream and desire, to the acknowledgement of the
tender

Of these, the inarticulate, like angels whose tongues of fire
Speak only of Heaven; like these, the dumb children
Play on our bare earth, our back yards, our floors,
Grow on our soil like plants, like puzzled beautiful flowers.

Who remember the tides of Heavenly light, and the salutation
Of waving in the fields on the celestial day.
These are the flowers we gather, that our desire grows,
Springing from the stars to the soil our love allows.

In the broken house they play; in the garden among the ruins
They coo like doves or pigeons for pieces of snapped brick;
They crawl among wreckage on the sands, at the sea's edge
They sprawl where wind and wave make smooth the bright
pillage.

Familiar are the black wings that come between them and the
sun;
The black hand that explodes, that is stronger than a mother's
arm;

Familiar the monstrous crow, big as tar barrel.
These children are rocked out of sleep by their father's quarrel.

Out of our desire they come, from the hands of lovers
Stretching towards Heaven to pluck a growing blessing;
Out of the world's desire to feel the blood in its veins,
To spring as the corn springs, to clamber as the vines

With outspread arms for the sun across the breast of the earth;
To feel to the roots, to suck, to imbibe the full draught;
Declaring to its mountains, 'I am world that survives,
In them I acknowledge myself. I acknowledge that man lives.'

Out of our desire they come, from the fire that forces us
Out our lovers, the flowers, that we must gather and nourish.
And for them must the world be woman; heart turns to the
Heavenly Mother,
Who sets us in a cradle of peace, whose hand is a firm rocker.

Anne Ridler

NOW AS THEN

When under Edward or Henry the English armies,
Whose battles are brocade to us and stiff in tapestries,
On a green and curling sea set out for France,
The Holy Ghost moved the sails, the lance
Was hung with glory, and in all sincerity
Poets cried 'God will grant to us the victory'.
For us, who by proxy inflicted gross oppression,
Among whom the humblest have some sins of omission,
War is not simple: in more or less degree
All are guilty, though some will suffer unjustly.
Can we say mass to dedicate our bombs?
Yet those earlier English, for all their psalms
Were marauders, had less provocation than we,
And the causes of war were as mixed and hard to see.
And since of two evils our victory would be the less,
And coming soon, leave some strength for peace,
Hopeful like Minot and the rest, we pray:
'Lord, turn us again, confer on us victory.'

AT PARTING

Since we through war awhile must part
Sweetheart, and learn to lose
Daily use
Of all that satisfied our heart:
Lay up those secrets and those powers
Wherewith you pleased and cherished me these two years:

Now we must draw, as plants would,
On tubers stored in a better season,
Our honey and heaven;
Only our love can store such food.
Is this to make a god of absence?
A new-born monster to steal our sustenance?

We cannot quite cast out lack and pain.
Let him remain – what he may devour
We can well spare:
He never can tap this, the true vein.
I have no words to tell you what you were,
But when you are sad, think, Heaven could give no more.

BEFORE SLEEP

Now that you lie
   In London afar,
And may sleep longer
   Though lonelier,
For I shall not wake you
   With a nightmare,
Heaven plant such peace in us
As if no parting stretched between us.

The world revolves
   And is evil;
God's image is
   Wormeaten by the devil;
May the good angel
   Have no rival
By our beds, and we lie curled
At the sound unmoving heart of the world.

In our good nights
   When we were together,
We made, in that stillness
   Where we loved each other,
A new being, of both
   Yet above either:
So, when I cannot share your sleep,
Into this being, half yours, I creep.

Patricia M. Saunders

ONE OF OUR AIRCRAFT FAILED TO RETURN

In the squadron you will be replaced
by another young officer,
open-faced
with a good nerve,
dash of initiative
eager to serve. . . .

. . . and in the mess
another such
gay and modest will confess
there are often moments when courage fails
in spite of purple ribbons
and comrades' tales. . . .

. . . Only on these acres of green
pasture-land dedicated by your forebears
could your passing mean
irreparable disaster
to the woman who loved you, the horse you rode,
the dog who called you master.

20TH CENTURY REQUIEM

None of us ever doubted
he was indeed the best of us,
more skilful in the art of living
than the rest of us.

His death was no pitiful drama
laboriously enacted before our eyes.
He died remotely beyond the horizon
as a comet or a meteor dies.

The cabled news was brief
but it shattered our world like shrapnel,
splintering our lives
with all the violence of a bursting shell.

We said (more from fear than from conviction)
'He would feel nothing, it was so swift,'
and with this comfortable fiction
gave fear short shrift.

Our unquestioned leader
it was so like him to go before us
into the mapless region of death
thereby diminishing the terror for us.

For however we may recoil
from the invisible torrent
we shall not be entirely fearful to follow on
into the unfathomable canyon where he has gone.

Myra Schneider

DRAWING A BANANA

(A Memory of Childhood during the War)

Forty of us looked longingly at the yellow finger
Plumped, curved, bearing strange black marks.
The word 'banana' purred insistently round the classroom.
Our teacher, furrowed by severity as much as age,
Smiled slightly, then mounted her trophy on a box for us
To draw with thick pencil on thin, grey page.

We licked our lips in hope. Dimly we thought
The banana would be shared, perhaps that it would stretch
Like the bread and fish once did among the multitude.
A clearer idea flowered: it was for one child to win.
The bloom was nipped as it emerged our teacher meant to keep
The prize herself, and all alone to strip its golden skin.

It was boring drawing that banana. My leaden lines
Smudged with rubbings out didn't resemble the fruit taunting
My hungry eyes. I couldn't quite remember seeing
A 'live' banana before – there was a war to fight
And grown-ups said we had to go without and make do.
Yet if I closed my eyes I could conjure up a feast of a sight:

A window of violet-iced cakes and chocolates heaped
On silver trays belonging to a piece of magic time.
As far as my certainty stretched back war enveloped all.
War meant sombre ships sliding slowly down the Clyde,
Sirens, snuggling with cocoa in the cupboard beneath the stairs
Though the only bomb that fell was on the moors and no one
  died.

Fear couldn't touch me for I knew with crystal-cut clarity
Our side was in the right and therefore bound to win.
Yet my parents frowned and talked in hushed gloom
By the crackling wireless. If the Germans march through France
Never mind, I urged. With God fighting for England
It was in the fields of Hell that the fiend Hitler would dance.

I was proved right in the end, but long before then
My belief was crumbling in that lost paradise, peace.
I dreamed, daydreamed the war had ended. Warships
Decked out in scarlet streamers docked at our little pier,
Soldiers surged down the gangways to crowds in gaudy clothes,
Music reeled from radios – there'd be no more news to hear.

Ice-cream parlours would grow pink and come alive
To sell real ices not those fadings on the walls.
Rationing would end – I'd buy chocolate drops in mounds.
Bulging hands of bananas would hang in the greengrocer's shop
But instead of drawing stupidly I'd bite into a bunch
And no grim-faced grown-up would shout at me to stop.

E. J. Scovell

DAYS DRAWING IN

The days fail: night broods over afternoon:
And at my child's first drink beyond the night
Her skin is silver in the early light.
Sweet the grey morning and the raiders gone.

A WARTIME STORY

Florence, her husband two years overseas,
In summer knew herself pregnant by another,
Her passing lover, an airman, and at Christmas
Alone one morning before light gave birth.
This is the story she told the police:
'It was born alive. I wrapped it in a blanket.
I laid it under the bed. At half-past nine
I went down and made breakfast for the children.
When I came up it was dead. I left it
For two days in the blanket out of sight,
Then late at night made up the fire and poured
Paraffin on and burnt it.'

Agent of fate:
Large head and feeble neck and fakir limbs;
Blind eyes once opened on blood and closed in night,
And faint life, mere sentience of pain, soon ended:
Still you played your part, accuser, evidence
To be destroyed; and when all was uncovered
Lived on as trouble and sorrow to the living.

Did she act in pain? Did she love the baby at all
Living or dead? Did she draw the incurable lightning-
Pang of pity? Did she remember the spring
And think of the father? Or was there only fear,
Anxiety and her body's sick exhaustion?
We have not seen her face.

But we can imagine
The baby's face, haggard with birth; the head
Cast in the womb and flattened in the cervix;
And the shadow of the womb lingering, the shadow
Of sleep, the haunting of non-existence still
On the flower of the body, perfect in every part.

Beauty, life, infinite infolding; soul
Nameless, sex unrecorded, agent of fate
Like a stone dropped in the pool of grosser lives
That leaves its stir and itself sinks out of sight,
Deep, one-way, plumb-straight, heavy from hand of God:
In your whirlpool you draw our hearts down after,
But we do not find you.

Sheila Shannon

ON A CHILD ASLEEP IN A TUBE SHELTER

(London, March 1944)

He sleeps undreaming; all his world
Furled in its winter sheath; green leaves
And pale small buds fast folded lie
As he lies curled as if his mother's arms
   Held him and tenderly kept the world away.

His eyelids draw soft shadows down
And ward away the harsh lights' glare;
His parted lips draw breath as though
Breathing grass-scented, cool, hill-country air
   He tasted not this subterranean draught.

Indifferent trains roll in and out;
Indifferent crowds, who stand or stroll
Wearily up and down, who shout
Against the echoing din: yet he sleeps still,
   Deep in oblivion beyond their farthest call.

Whose searchlights finger stars but pass
Looking for something else; whose town
Sleeps with its eyes half-closed, its ears
Alert for war's alarms, whose troubled dreams
   Stir the light surface of night's uneasy sleep.

The child is hidden underground
Yet Sleep still lovingly seeks him out
And keeps him tenderly till dawn.
Above, men listen for the roll of guns
   And sighs lie on the lips of the drowsy watchers.

Edith Sitwell

STILL FALLS THE RAIN

The Raids, 1940. Night and Dawn

Still falls the Rain –
Dark as the world of man, black as our loss –
Blind as the nineteen hundred and forty nails
Upon the Cross.

Still falls the Rain
With a sound like the pulse of the heart that is changed to the hammer-beat
In the Potter's Field, and the sound of the impious feet

On the Tomb:
Still falls the Rain
In the Field of Blood where the small hopes breed and the human brain
Nurtures its greed, that worm with the brow of Cain.

Still falls the Rain
At the feet of the Starved Man hung upon the Cross.
Christ that each day, each night, nails there, have mercy on us –
On Dives and on Lazarus:
Under the Rain the sore and the gold are as one.

Still falls the Rain –
Still falls the Blood from the Starved Man's wounded Side:
He bears in His Heart all wounds, – those of the light that died,
The last faint spark
In the self-murdered heart, the wounds of the sad uncomprehending dark,
The wounds of the baited bear, –
The blind and weeping bear whom the keepers beat
On his helpless flesh . . . the tears of the hunted hare.

Still falls the Rain –
Then – O Ile leape up to my God: who pulles me doune –
See, see where Christ's blood streames in the firmament:
It flows from the Brow we nailed upon the tree
Deep to the dying, to the thirsting heart

That holds the fires of the world, – dark-smirched with pain
As Caesar's laurel crown.

Then sounds the voice of One who like the heart of man
Was once a child who among beasts has lain –
'Still do I love, still shed my innocent light, my Blood, for thee.'

Margery Smith

FOR FREDA

More than a year has reeled and clamoured by
Since you and I
Struggled with frost and thoughts on Hampstead Heath;
Our words cut sharply as November breath
That, with a windy shout,
Tumbled the last dead leaves about.

It seems but yesterday we walked in Kew
Through copper-dripping trees and long lawns of dew.
All that is past, and yet at times I know
We have been together, in the snow,
And by the sad slow winter streams
Of dreams.

All that is past. Another year will reel and clatter down
On field and town;
A year loud with battle on the seas,
Of thunder in the cities, on the breeze
The iron birds will come, first like a breath,
Then roaring – anger swooping – then death,

Death for the innocent – but is that true?
Am I innocent, are you?
But who may say?
The coming years must judge; our day
Still holds its wrath; the years
Alone can give the answer to our fears.

THE UNKNOWN WARRIOR SPEAKS

You who softly wane into a shadow,
Whom long night-winds have gently trampled by,
Who pick all flowers that you wish from meadows,
Who think and dream and sing,
And undespairing swing
To lifelessness –
You sleep forgotten when you die.

My dreams were pushed at noon into a gun;
My songs were bombs, and human blood my river;
And fighting I was hurled towards the sun
For liberty and you.
But at that moment grew
A loveliness in death,
For I have life forever.

Stevie Smith

VOICES AGAINST ENGLAND IN THE NIGHT

'England, you had better go,
There is nothing else that you ought to do,
You lump of survival value, you are too slow.

'England, you have been here too long,
And the songs you sing are the songs you sung
On a braver day. Now they are wrong.

'And as you sing the sliver slips from your lips,
And the governing garment sits ridiculously on your hips.
It is a pity that you are still too cunning to make slips.'

Dr Goebbels, that is the point,
You are a few years too soon with your jaunt,
Time and the moment is not yet England's daunt.

Yes, dreaming Germany, with your Urge and Night,
You must go down before English and American might.
It is well, it is well, cries the peace kite.

Perhaps England our darling will recover her lost thought
We must think sensibly about our victory and not be distraught,
Perhaps America will have an idea, and perhaps not.

But they cried: Could not England, once the world's best,
Put off her governing garment and be better dressed
In a shroud, a shroud? O history turn thy pages fast!

Sarah Stafford

THE UNBORN

Will the tree bloom again, and the red field
Suffer the soft invasion of the wheat?
Will the bomb-crater be a standing pool
Where little boys catch minnows? Will the town
Cover its scars and ring its bells again?
Shall we have peace at morning, and at noon
No gun to shake the quiet of the hills?
And in the dusty lane, no bullets' hail,
Only the small, sweet clamour of the birds?
All this shall come, and we have peace again,
A haunted peace, for we have done a thing
The ancient gods, in all their wrath, had wept for.
We have robbed the world of a myriad human faces
And twice a myriad beauty-making hands.
For in the bodies of the slain in battle
And in the dark wombs of the mourning women
Lie lovely nations, never to be born.
Some, it may be, better unborn, but some
Irreparable losses, and for these,
Not in eternity can we atone.
Not in eternity can we remember
The song unsung, nor read the word unwritten,
Nor see the coloured landscape through the eyes
And the warm minds of artists never born.
So, when a man lays down his lusty life
To save his land, he says with dying breath,
'Here, people, since you need it, is my life
And my son's life, yes, and my son's son's life,
And my wife's joy, and all our sums of joy
And God knows what of richness and delight
That might have flowed from me. You make me now,
In death, a sad, perpetual Abraham –
Slaying my son, slaying my son for ever.
You know there is no thicket and no ram
And no reprieving angel at my side.'

Ruth Tomalin

INVASION SPRING

Where purple cuckoo-clappers quake
within their green translucent shrine,
and cobra-headed ferns awake,
the sullen mighty tanks recline.

Young shepherds sleep beside their flock,
or watch the stormy skies all night,
where brown owls with soft voices mock
great bands of darker birds in flight.

Like old calm shepherds of the fell
these know and call their lambs by name –
Susannah, Charmer, Cheyenne Belle,
Calamity and Texas Dame.

All Sussex flows with silver blood
from wounded white anemones,
while flowers in dark remembered mud
lie drowned among the waiting trees.

Here light words die as soldiers dream
beneath green hedges in the sun,
and see their twentieth April gleam,
who dare not hope for twenty-one.

1944

Catherine Brewster Toosey

COLOUR SYMPHONY

The coloured nights
have yellow and blue long lights
splintered by air-fire
on negative whites
backgrounding black-snapped
scarred trees
static.

In the mornings
there are planes on dray-biers
metal-grey moths crumpled
signed each with a white edged
black grave-cross:
these days
are a diary-film drama
coloured symphony
photographic
blast and bomb smash
death
and flame
magnetic
passing. . . .

Margaret Wainwright

O SUSANNA

O Susanna, Susanna, don't you cry –
It's 1917 and you'll
Have a husband by and by.
He's coming from the Messines Ridge,
Susanna, don't you cry.

O Susanna, Susanna, don't you cry –
It's 1933 and you
Have children who rely
On what you can scrape up for them
From a dole that's running dry.

O Susanna, now, Susanna, don't you cry,
Your son is just on twenty, and
It's time for him to die
In a blazing fighter-bomber like
A comet down the sky.

O Susanna, now, Susanna, don't you cry,
With seven little grandchildren
All growing up so high:
In peacetime with the atom bomb,
Susanna, don't you cry.

Sylvia Townsend Warner

ROAD 1940

Why do I carry, she said,
This child that is no child of mine?
Through the heat of the day it did nothing but fidget and whine,
Now it snuffles under the dew and the cold star-shine,
And lies across my heart heavy as lead,
Heavy as the dead.

Why did I lift it, she said,
Out of its cradle in the wheel-tracks?
On the dusty road burdens have melted like wax,
Soldiers have thrown down their rifles, misers slipped their
  packs:
Yes, and the woman who left it there has sped
With a lighter tread.

Though I should save it, she said,
What have I saved for the world's use?
If it grow to hero it will die or let loose
Death, or to hireling, nature already is too profuse
Of such, who hope and are disinherited,
Plough, and are not fed.

But since I've carried it, she said,
So far I might as well carry it still.
If we ever should come to kindness someone will
Pity me perhaps as the mother of a child so ill,
Grant me even to lie down on a bed;
Give me at least bread.

Dorothy Wellesley

MILK BOY

There are no more tears for the body to weep with.

Early this morning at the break of day,
A boy of sixteen went out for the milking
Up on the white farm alone on the hill,
With a single white candle upheld by his hand,
Carrying his pail through the air so still.

Then came the Nazi, knowing the white farm there,
The hour of milking white heifers of morning.

There lay the red pools, with the milk pools mingling
O there in the sun – in the red sun arising,
The white boy, the white candle, the white heifer
Dying. . . .

1942

SPRING IN THE PARK

(London 1919: 1943)

The sudden crocuses start up, erupt
Like flames along the stark uncoloured grass,
Striped mauves, profounder purples, bright, abrupt,
Strong copper golds. And as the wounded pass,
Flayed, broken, bled, the snow-wind and the snow
Gather and pause and charge the earth again,
Rush the dark sanctity of drought below
The cedar tree's long levels, plane on plane
Scour the twig-littered lawn, and they, the wounded, watch
Crocuses blow to shuddering fire, cross over
The blanched grass limping, blue patch on patch.

There is a woman who has lost her lover, –
She hunts the spring flowers mutely since he died.
And there a boy, disfigured, daily told, –
When the kind friend has winced and looked aside, –
He lost his face to build 'an Age of Gold'.

Ursula Vaughan Williams

PENELOPE

Certain parting does not wait its hour
for separation; too soon the shadow lies
upon the heart and chokes the voice, its power
drives on the minutes, it implies
tomorrow while today's still here.

They sat by firelight and his shadow fell
for the last time, she thought, black patterning gold
sharp on the firelit wall. So, to compel
the evening to outlast the morning's cold
dawn by the quayside and the unshed tears,

she took a charred twig from the hearth and drew
the outline of his shadow on the wall.
'These were his features, this the hand I knew.'
She heard her voice saying the words through all
the future days of solitude and fear.

Mary Wilson

OXFORD IN WARTIME

The silenced bells hang mutely in the towers,
The stained-glass windows have been taken down
To Wales, to shelter underneath the mountains;
And battledress has shouldered-out the gown.
And undergraduates waiting for their call-up,
And feeling restless and dissatisfied
Are fighting with Australians in the Milk Bar;
Yet soon they will be serving side by side.
Flapping in tattered fragments from the billboards,
Torn posters advertise an old Commem,
And some who danced all night have gone for ever –
The Roll of Honour will remember them.
The colleges are full of Civil Servants
Trucking and jiving when the day is done,
And as the evening mists rise over Isis,
The R.A.F. flood in from Abingdon
To the King's Arms, to play bar billiards;
Laughing and talking, flirting, drinking beer
No shadow from the future clouds their faces,
Only a heightened sense of danger near.
The pencil search-lights swing across the darkness,
The bombers throb above through driving rain,
We know that Woolton pie is on the menu
In the new British Restaurant at the Plain.
So tiring of the dreary wartime rations,
To dine at the George Restaurant we go,
Where high above the scene of shabby splendour
The punkas waver slowly to and fro.
The Barrel is rolled out beneath my window,
Deep purple always falls with falling night,
And here, and in the enemy's encampments
Lili Marlène stands by the blacked-out light.
She shines a tissued torch upon her nylons
And ties her hair up in a Victory Roll.
Washing is hanging in the Fellows' Garden,
Evacuees live in the Metropole.

And in the crowded daytime roads of Oxford,
The shifting costumes make a masquerade
As men and women officers, all polished
Mingle with cloaked exquisites from the Slade.
In blue suits and red ties, the walking wounded
Hobble with sticks to help their bandaged feet,
And prisoners-of-war, with yellow circles
On their brown battledress, dig in the street.
And we all live as if there's no tomorrow –
Indeed, for some of us, there will not be –
And 'til the bugle calls us to the conflict
We sit in the Cadena, drinking tea.

Those wartime years have gone, and left no traces,
Fresh tides of youth have swept them all away;
New buildings have arisen by the river,
And there are few who think of yesterday;
Yet sometimes, in the middle of September
Though Spitfires scream no more across the sky,
As dusk comes down, you cannot see the pavement
Where ghosts in blue are walking down the High.

Diana Witherby

CASUALTY

Death stretched down two hands,
One on desert sands
Shut his eyes. The other in her head
Opened the third eye of ruin; instead
Of doubt, which veiled it, certainty now gives it sight,
Staring dark and twitching when she sleeps at night,
When she wakes turning her, indifferent, from light.

Sometimes looking through a door into a sunny room, cold,
Full of furniture, but empty except for herself, old
In the mirror. Sometimes resting on fields flowing their green
  gold
Flowers, giving her an illusion of summer, but her thawing tear
Freezes quickly in the eternal ice of confirmed fear.
Sometimes, drifting along the canal of fatigue, he seems near,
The eye is closing – then suddenly starts in her brain,
Opens – He is gone. She, with walls, iron-cloured rain,
Railings silhouetted either side, is alone again.

We, who for our own comfort, imagined that a grief,
Could be smoothed and stroked by time to its relief,
Looking at her face, know now that only their brief
Past stands. The sun has equal entrance there
With mist or wind. We move in talking where
Gates stood – but voices fade,
Transfixed, in her stone shade.

Elizabeth Wyse

From AUSCHWITZ

What big heavy doors!
Strange, lingering odour,
Faint but still here . . . strong disinfectant.
'Stand round the shower point'.
Wait for the water. Don't think about the crowd.
They don't notice your degradation.
They can't see your shaved head from all the rest!

My God! . . . They're locking those bloody great doors!
Why? . . . It can't be!
No, the water will come in a minute.
Don't cry, just be patient,
It will be all over very soon.

There's a noise – up there.
He's lifting that grate.
All eyes watching, wondering.
No sound.
What are those pellets? . . . Dry disinfectant.
Sulphur!!?

Gas! Gas! Gas! Panic!
The screams, the clutching,
Pulling, scrambling.
The total terror of realisation.

Timeless minutes climbing and scrambling.
Families forgotten. Self preservation.
Flesh on flesh – clutching and tearing.
Gas, screams, death . . . silence.

Acknowledgements

Scars upon my Heart

I am most grateful to all those who have helped me, in various ways, to complete this work. In particular I thank Alan Young and Michael Redhead, who were the first to view my selection with a critical eye; Victor Schwarz, who 'found' the title; H. J. D. Cole, Stephen Dobell, Gordon Phillips (Archivist, Times Newspapers Ltd), Charles Seaton (Librarian, *Spectator*) and Mrs E. A. Stapleforth, all of whom went to some trouble to assist with certain biographical notes on the poets.

Permission to reprint copyright poems in this book is gratefully acknowledged. Apologies are offered to those copyright-holders whom it has proved impossible to locate.

Marian Allen: 'The Raiders' and 'The Wind on the Downs' from *The Wind on the Downs*, published 1918 by Humphreys.

Lilian M. Anderson: 'Leave in 1917' from *Contemporary Devonshire and Cornwall Poetry*, edited by S. Fowler Wright, published 1930 by S. Fowler Wright.

Pauline Barrington: ' "Education" ' from *Poems Written during the Great War 1914–1918*, edited by Bertram Lloyd, published 1918 by George Allen & Unwin Ltd. Reprinted by permission of George Allen & Unwin Ltd.

Madeline Ida Bedford: 'Munition Wages' and 'The Parson's Job' from *The Young Captain*, published 1917 by Erskine Macdonald Ltd.

Maud Anna Bell: 'From a Trench' from *A Treasury of War Poetry*, edited by G. H. Clarke, published 1919 by Hodder & Stoughton Ltd. Reprinted by permission of *The Times*.

Nora Bomford: 'Drafts' from *Poems of a Pantheist*, published 1918 by Chatto & Windus Ltd.

Sybil Bristowe: 'Over the Top' from *The Lyceum Book of War Verse*, edited by A. E. Macklin, published 1918 by Erskine Macdonald Ltd.

Vera Brittain: 'The Lament of the Demobilised' from *Oxford Poetry 1920*, published 1920 by B. H. Blackwell, Oxford.

'Perhaps—' and 'To My Brother' from *Verses of a V.A.D.*, published 1918 by Erskine Macdonald Ltd. Reprinted by permission of Mr Paul Berry, Literary Executor of the Estate of the late Vera Brittain.

May Wedderburn Cannan: 'Lamplight', 'Rouen', 'Since They Have Died' and 'Love, 1916' from *In War Time*, published 1917 by B. H. Blackwell, Oxford. Reprinted by permission of Mr James C. Slater.

Isabel Constance Clarke: 'Anniversary of the Great Retreat' from *The Pathway of Dreams*, published 1919 by Sands & Co. Ltd.

Margaret Postgate Cole: 'The Falling Leaves' and 'Afterwards' from *Poems*, published 1918 by George Allen & Unwin Ltd. 'Praematuri' and 'The Veteran' from *An Anthology of War Poems*, edited by Frederick Brereton, published 1930 by William Collins & Co. Ltd. Reprinted by permission of Mr H. J. D. Cole.

Mary Gabrielle Collins: 'Women at Munition Making' from *Branches unto the Sea*, published 1916 by Erskine Macdonald Ltd.

Alice Corbin: 'Fallen' from *Poems of the Great War*, edited by J. W. Cunliffe, published 1916 by The Macmillan Company, New York. Reprinted by Books for Libraries Press. Distributed by Arno Press, Inc.

Nancy Cunard: 'Zeppelins' from *Outlaws*, published 1921 by Elkin Mathews. Reprinted by permission of Mr A. R. A. Hobson on behalf of The Estate of the late Nancy Cunard.

Elizabeth Daryush: 'Flanders Fields' and 'Unknown Warrior' from *Verses*, published 1930 by Oxford University Press. 'For a Survivor of the Mesopotamian Campaign' from *Verses: Third Book*, published 1933 by Oxford University Press. 'Subalterns' from *Verses: Fourth Book*, published 1934 by Oxford University Press. Reprinted by permission of Mr A. A. Daryush.

Helen Dircks: 'After Bourlon Wood' and 'London in War' from *Passenger*, published 1920 by Chatto & Windus Ltd. Reprinted by permission of the author and Chatto & Windus.

Eva Dobell: 'Pluck', 'Gramophone Tunes' and 'Night Duty' from *A Bunch of Cotswold Grasses*, published 1919 by Arthur H. Stockwell Ltd. Reprinted by permission of Mr P. H. M. Dobell.

Helen Parry Eden: 'A Volunteer' from *Coal and Candlelight*, published 1918 by The Bodley Head.

Gabrielle Elliot: 'Pierrot Goes to War' from *A Treasury of War Poetry, 2nd Series,* edited by G. H. Clarke, published 1919 by Houghton Mifflin Company, New York. Reprinted by permission of The New York Times Company.

Eleanor Farjeon: 'Easter Monday' from *First and Second Love,* published 1959 by Oxford University Press. 'Peace' and 'Now That You Too' from *Sonnets and Poems,* published 1918 by B. H. Blackwell, Oxford. Reprinted by permission of David Higham Associates Ltd.

S. Gertrude Ford: ' "A Fight to a Finish" ' and 'Nature in War-Time' from *A Fight to a Finish,* published 1917 by C. W. Daniel & Co. Ltd. 'The Tenth Armistice Day' from *The England of My Dream,* published 1928 by C. W. Daniel & Co. Ltd.

Elizabeth Chandler Forman: 'The Three Lads' from *War Verse,* edited by Frank Foxcroft, published 1919 by The Thomas Y. Crowell Company, New York. Reprinted by permission of The Thomas Y. Crowell Company, New York.

Lillian Gard: 'Her "Allowance"!' from *The Country Life Anthology of Verse*, edited by Peter A. Graham, published 1915 by *Country Life* and Newnes. Reprinted by permission of The Hamlyn Publishing Group Ltd.

Muriel Elsie Graham: 'The Lark above the Trenches' and 'The Battle of the Swamps' from *Collected Poems,* published 1930 by Williams & Norgate Ltd. Reprinted by permission of Ernest Benn Ltd.

Nora Griffiths: 'The Wykhamist' from *The Country Life Anthology of Verse,* edited by Peter A. Graham, published 1915 by *Country Life* and Newnes. Reprinted by permission of The Hamlyn Publishing Group Ltd.

Diana Gurney: 'The Fallen' from *Verses,* published 1926 by Cayme Press.

Cicely Hamilton: 'Non-Combatant' from *Poems of the Great War,* edited by J. W. Cunliffe, published 1916 by The Macmillan Company, New York. Reprinted by Books for Libraries Press. Distributed by Arno Press, Inc.

Helen Hamilton: 'The Ghouls', 'The Jingo-Woman' and 'The Romancing Poet' from *Napoo!*, published 1918 by B. H. Blackwell, Oxford.

Ada May Harrison: 'New Year, 1916' from *Cambridge Poets, 1914–1920*, edited by Edward Davison, published 1920 by Heffer, Cambridge.

Mary H. J. Henderson: 'An Incident' from *The Lyceum Book of War Verse*, edited by Alys Eyre Macklin, published 1918 by Erskine Macdonald Ltd.

Agnes Grozier Herbertson: 'Airman, R.F.C.' from *This Is the Hour*, published 1942 by Fortune Press. Reprinted by permission of Charles Skilton Ltd. 'The Seed-Merchant's Son' from *The Quiet Heart*, published 1919 by Elkin Mathews.

May Herschel-Clarke: ' "For Valour" ' and ' "Nothing to Report" ' from *Behind the Firing Line*, published 1917 by Erskine Macdonald Ltd.

Teresa Hooley: 'A War Film' from *Songs of All Seasons*, published 1927 by Jonathan Cape Ltd. Reprinted by permission of The Estate of the late Teresa Hooley, and Jonathan Cape Ltd.

Elinor Jenkins: 'Dulce Et Decorum?' from *Poems; Last Poems*, published 1921 by Sidgwick & Jackson Ltd. Reprinted by permission of Sidgwick & Jackson Ltd.

Anna Gordon Keown: 'Reported Missing' from *War Verse*, edited by Frank Foxcroft, published 1919 by The Thomas Y. Crowell Company, New York. Reprinted by permission of The Thomas Y. Crowell Company, New York.

Margery Lawrence: 'The Lost Army' and 'Transport of Wounded in Mesopotamia, 1917' from *Fourteen to Forty-Eight*, published 1949 by Robert Hale Ltd. Reprinted by permission of The Estate of the late Margery Lawrence, and Laurence Pollinger Ltd.

Winifred M. Letts: 'Casualty', 'Screens' and 'What Reward?' from *The Spires of Oxford*, published 1917 by E. P. Dutton, New York. 'The Deserter' from *Hallowe'en and Poems of the War*, published 1916 by Smith, Elder & Co. Reprinted by permission of John Murray (Publishers) Ltd.

Olive E. Lindsay: 'Despair' from *A Little Rhyme*, published 1925 by Oliver & Boyd, Edinburgh.

Amy Lowell: 'Convalescence' from *The Complete Poetical Works of Amy Lowell*, published 1955 by Houghton Mifflin Company. Reprinted by permission of Houghton Mifflin Company.

Rose Macaulay: 'Picnic' and 'The Shadow' from *Three Days*, published 1919 by Constable & Co. Ltd. Reprinted by permission of A. D. Peters & Co. Ltd.

Nina Macdonald: 'Sing a Song of War-Time' from *War-Time Nursery Rhymes*, published 1918 by Routledge & Kegan Paul Ltd. Reprinted by permission of Routledge & Kegan Paul Ltd.

Florence Ripley Mastin: 'At the Movies' from *A Treasury of War Poetry, 2nd Series*, edited by G. H. Clarke, published 1919 by Houghton Mifflin Company. Reprinted by permission of The New York Times Company.

Charlotte Mew: 'The Cenotaph', 'May, 1915' and 'June, 1915' from *Collected Poems*, published 1953 by Gerald Duckworth & Co. Ltd. Reprinted by permission of Gerald Duckworth & Co. Ltd.

Alice Meynell: 'Lord, I Owe Thee a Death' and 'Summer in England, 1914' from *Poems. Complete Edition*, published 1940 by Burns, Oates & Washbourne Ltd.

Ruth Comfort Mitchell: 'He Went for a Soldier' from *Poems of the Great War*, edited by J. W. Cunliffe, published 1916 by The Macmillan Company, New York. Reprinted by Books for Libraries Press. Distributed by Arno Press, Inc.

Harriet Monroe: 'On the Porch' from *Poems of the Great War*, edited by J. W. Cunliffe, published 1916 by The Macmillan Company, New York. Reprinted by Books for Libraries Press. Distributed by Arno Press, Inc.

Edith Nesbit: 'The Fields of Flanders' and 'Spring in War-Time' from *Many Voices*, published 1922 by Hutchinson & Co. Ltd.

Eileen Newton: 'Last Leave' and 'Revision' from *Lamps in the Valley*, published 1927 by Elkin Mathews & Marrot.

Eleanour Norton: 'In a Restaurant, 1917' from *Magic*,

published 1922 by Wilson, London.

Carola Oman: 'Ambulance Train 30' and 'Brussels, 1919' from *The Menin Road*, published 1919 by Hodder & Stoughton Ltd. Reprinted by permission of Mr P. R. O. Stuart.

May O'Rourke: 'The Minority: 1917' from *West Wind Days*, published 1918 by Erskine Macdonald Ltd.

Emily Orr: 'A Recruit from the Slums' from *A Harvester of Dreams*, published 1922 by Burns, Oates & Washbourne Ltd.

Jessie Pope: 'The Call' and 'Socks' from *War Poems*, published 1915 by Grant Richards. 'The Nut's Birthday' from *More War Poems*, published 1915 by Grant Richards. 'War Girls' from *Simple Rhymes for Stirring Times*, published 1916 by C. Arthur Pearson. Reprinted by permission of The Hamlyn Publishing Group Ltd.

Inez Quilter: ' "Sall" ' from *A Book of Poems for the Blue Cross Fund*, published 1917 by Jarrolds Publishers (London) Ltd.

Dorothy Una Ratcliffe: 'Remembrance Day in the Dales' from *Singing Rivers*, published 1922 by The Bodley Head. Reprinted by permission of Mrs Ludi Horenstein.

Ursula Roberts ('Susan Miles'): 'The Cenotaph' from *Annotations* by 'Susan Miles', published 1922 by Oxford University Press. Reprinted by permission of Oxford University Press.

Margaret Sackville: 'A Memory' from *The Pageant of War*, published 1916 by Simpkin, Marshall, Hamilton, Kent & Co. Ltd. 'Sacrament' from *Collected Poems*, published 1939 by Martin Secker.

Aimee Byng Scott: 'July 1st, 1916' from *The Road to Calais*, published 1919 by Thacker.

May Sinclair: 'Field Ambulance in Retreat' from *King Albert's Book*, edited by Hall Caine, published 1914 by Hodder & Stoughton Ltd. Reprinted by permission of Curtis Brown Ltd.

Edith Sitwell: 'The Dancers' from *Clowns' Houses*, published 1918 by B. H. Blackwell, Oxford. Reprinted by permission of David Higham Associates on behalf of the Estate of the late Dame Edith Sitwell.

Cicily Fox Smith: 'The Convalescent' from *Fighting Men*, published 1916 by Elkin Mathews.

Marie Carmichael Stopes: 'Night on the Shore' from *The Lyceum Book of War Verse*, edited by Alys Eyre Macklin, published 1918 by Erskine Macdonald Ltd.

Muriel Stuart: 'Forgotten Dead, I Salute You' from *Poems*, published 1922 by William Heinemann Ltd. Reprinted by permission of Mrs E. A. Stapleforth.

Millicent Sutherland: 'One Night' from *Lest We Forget*, edited by H. B. Elliott, published 1915 by Jarrolds Publishers (London) Ltd. Reprinted by permission of Elizabeth, Countess of Sutherland.

C.A.L.T.: 'Y.M.C.A.' from *A Pocketful of Rye*, privately printed [1916?] by Martin & Sturt, Farnham.

Sara Teasdale: 'Spring in War-Time' from *Poems of the Great War*, edited by J. W. Cunliffe, published 1916 by The Macmillan Company, New York. Reprinted by Books for Libraries Press. Distributed by Arno Press, Inc. ' "There Will Come Soft Rains" ' from *Collected Poems of Sara Teasdale*, copyright 1920 by Macmillan Publishing Co. Inc., New York, renewed 1948 by Mamie T. Wheless. Reprinted by permission of Macmillan Publishing Co. Inc., New York.

Lesbia Thanet: 'In Time of War' from *War Verse*, edited by Frank Foxcroft, published 1919 by The Thomas Y. Crowell Company, New York. Reprinted by permission of The Thomas Y. Crowell Company, New York.

Aelfrida Tillyard: 'Invitation au Festin' and 'A Letter from Ealing Broadway Station' from *The Garden and the Fire*, published 1916 by Heffer, Cambridge.

Iris Tree: 'Of all who died in silence far away . . .' and 'And afterwards, when honour has made good . . .' from *Poems*, published 1920 by The Bodley Head.

Alys Fane Trotter: 'The Hospital Visitor' from *Houses and Dreams*, published 1924 by B. H. Blackwell, Oxford.

Katharine Tynan: 'The Broken Soldier' from *Collected Poems*, published 1930 by Macmillan & Co. Ltd. 'A Girl's Song' and 'Joining the Colours' from *Flower of Youth*, published 1918 by Sidgwick & Jackson Ltd. Reprinted by permission of The Society of Authors and Miss Pamela Hinkson.

Viviane Verne: 'Kensington Gardens' from *A Casket of Thoughts,* published 1916 by Simpkin, Marshall, Hamilton, Kent & Co. Ltd.

Alberta Vickridge: 'In a V.A.D. Pantry' from *The Sea Gazer,* published 1919 by Erskine Macdonald Ltd.

Mary Webb: 'Autumn, 1914' from *Fifty-One Poems,* published 1946 by Jonathan Cape Ltd. Reprinted by permission of The Executors of the Mary Webb Estate.

M. Winifred Wedgwood: 'The V.A.D. Scullery-Maid's Song' and 'Christmas, 1916' from *Verses of a V.A.D. Kitchen-Maid,* published 1917 by Gregory & Scott Ltd, Torquay.

Catherine Durning Whetham: 'The Poet and the Butcher' from *An Exeter Book of Verse,* published 1919 by Eland, Exeter.

Lucy Whitmell: 'Christ in Flanders' from *An Anthology of War Poems,* edited by Frederick Brereton, published 1930 by William Collins & Co. Ltd.

Margaret Adelaide Wilson: 'Gervais' from *A Treasury of War Poetry,* edited by G. H. Clarke, published 1919 by Hodder & Stoughton Ltd.

Marjorie Wilson: 'To Tony (Aged 3)' from *A Treasury of War Poetry, 2nd Series,* edited by G. H. Clarke, published 1919 by Houghton Mifflin Company, New York.

Acknowledgements

Chaos of the Night

I am indebted to all those who have assisted me, in various ways, to complete this anthology. Special thanks are due to the poets whose work is represented here – both for their poems and for their help in the compilation of biographical notes. Thanks are due also to the literary representatives of those poets who are now deceased. I am grateful to Catherine Lee and Mary Schwarz for their valuable comments on my selection, and to Howard Sergeant of Outposts Publications for his expert advice so generously given.

Valentine Ackland: '7 October, 1940', 'Black-Out' and 'Notes on Life at Home, February, 1942' from *The Nature of the Moment*, published 1973 by Chatto & Windus Ltd. Reprinted by permission of Susanna Pinney and William Maxwell and Chatto & Windus Ltd.

Mabel Esther Allan: 'I Saw a Broken Town' from *Poetry Quarterly*, Summer 1941. 'Immensity' from *Time to Go Back*, published 1972 by Abelard-Schuman Ltd. Reprinted by permission of the author.

Phyllis Shand Allfrey: 'Cunard Liner 1940' and 'Young Lady Dancing with Soldier' from *In Circles*, printed 1940 by Raven Press. Reprinted by permission of the author.

Mary Désirée Anderson: 'Harvest' and 'The Black-Out' from *Bow Bells Are Silent*, published 1943 by Williams & Norgate Ltd. Reprinted by permission of Sir Trenchard Cox.

Juliette de Bairacli-Levy: 'Killed in Action' from *The Willow Wreath*, published 1943 by De Bairacli-Levy. 'Threnode for Young Soldiers Killed in Action' from *The Yew Wreath*, published 1947 by Ian Allan Ltd. Reprinted by permission of the author.

Joan Barton: 'First News Reel: September 1939' from *A House under Old Sarum*, published 1981 by Harry Chambers/Peterloo Poets. Reprinted by permission of the author.

Joyce Barton: 'Epitaph on a Soldier'. Previously unpublished. Printed by permission of the author.

Rachael Bates: 'The Infinite Debt' and 'How Sweet the Night' from *Songs from a Lake*, published 1947 by Hutchinson & Co. Ltd.

Marjorie Battcock: 'The Refugee' from *Chiaroscuro*, published 1960 by Outposts Publications. Reprinted by permission of the author.

Vera Bax: 'To Richard, My Son' from *The Distaff Muse*, edited by Clifford Bax and Meum Stewart, published 1949 by Hollis & Carter Ltd. 'To Billy, My Son', previously unpublished. 'The Fallen' from *Anthology for Verse Speakers*, edited by E. Guy Pertwee, published 1950 by Samuel French Ltd. Reprinted by permission of Paul A. North, Literary Executor of the Estate of Vera Bax.

Mary Beadnell: 'Hiroshima' from *Dale's Feet*, published 1969 by Outposts Publications. Reprinted by permission of Outposts Publications and the author.

Audrey Beecham: 'Song' from *Poetry (London)*, November 1944. 'Ditty' from *New Statesman and Nation*, 29 April 1944. 'Eichmann' from *Different Weather*, published 1980 by The Weybrook Press. Reprinted by permission of the author.

Frances Bellerby: 'Invalided Home' and 'War Casualty in April' from *Plash Mill*, published 1946 by Peter Davies Ltd. Reprinted by permission of William Heinemann Ltd.

Elizabeth Berridge: 'Bombed Church' from *Triad One*, published 1946 by Dennis Dobson Ltd. Reprinted by permission of the author.

Marjorie Boulton: 'Spring Betrayed' from *Preliminaries*, published 1949 by Fortune Press. Reprinted by permission of the author and Charles Skilton Ltd.

Anne Bulley: 'Leave Poem' from *Selected Poems of Anne Bulley*, published 1980 by The Lomond Press. Reprinted by permission of The Lomond Press.

Christina Chapin: 'On a Bomb Heard through a Violin Concerto' from *Poems 1929–1941*, published 1941 by Shakespeare Head Press.

Sarah Churchill: 'The Bombers' and 'R.A.F.' from *The Empty Spaces*, published 1966 by Leslie Frewin Ltd. Reprinted by permission of Leslie Frewin.

Lois Clark: 'Flashback' from *The Dance of Remembered Days* published 1974 by Ver Poets. 'Picture from the Blitz' and 'Fly Past Alderney' from *Another Dimension*, published 1982 by Outposts Publications. Reprinted by permission of the author.

Alice Coats: 'Sky-Conscious' and 'The "Monstrous Regiment" ' from *Poems of the Land Army*, published 1945 by the *Land Girl*.

Marion Coleman: 'Monte Cassino 1945' from *Myself Is All I Have*, published 1969 by Outposts Publications. Reprinted by permission of the author.

Ellodë Collins: 'Cessation of War' from the *Spectator*. Reprinted by permission of the *Spectator*.

Frances Cornford: 'From a Letter to America on a Visit to Sussex: Spring 1942', 'Soldiers on the Platform', 'Casualties' and 'Autumn Blitz' from *Travelling Home*, published 1948 by Cresset Press. Reprinted by permission of Christopher Cornford and Hutchinson Publishing Group Ltd.

N. K. Cruickshank: 'Snowy Morning, 1940' and 'Enemy Action' from *In the Tower's Shadow*, published 1948 by Oxford University Press.

Elizabeth Daryush: 'War Tribunal' from *Collected Poems*, published 1976 by Carcanet New Press. Reprinted by permission of A. A. Daryush.

Barbara Catherine Edwards: 'A Wartime Maternity Ward' and 'Bomb Incident' from *Poems from Hospital*, published 1962 by Outposts Publications. Reprinted by permission of Outposts Publications and the author.

Ruth Evans: 'A Roman in Libya' from *War Poems from the 'Sunday Times'*, printed 1945 for private circulation.

Elaine Feinstein: 'A Quiet War in Leicester' from *The Magic Apple Tree*, published 1971 by Hutchinson. Reprinted by permission of Hutchinson Publishing Group Ltd.

Mabel Ferrett: 'John Douglas White' from *The Years of the Right Hand*, published 1975 by Hub Publications Ltd. 'Wartime Report Centre: Solo School', previously unpublished. Reprinted by permission of the author.

Olivia FitzRoy: 'Fleet Fighter', 'When He Is Flying' and 'Toast' from *Selected Poems*, privately published. Reprinted by permission of Viscount Daventry.

Karen Gershon: 'Home' and 'A Jew's Calendar' from *Selected Poems*, published 1966 by Victor Gollancz Ltd. Reprinted by permission of the author.

Beatrice R. Gibbs: 'The Bomber' from *War Poems from the 'Sunday Times'*, printed 1945 for private circulation.

Virginia Graham: '1939 Somewhere in England' and 'It's All Very Well Now' from *Consider the Years, 1938–1946*, published 1946 by Jonathan Cape Ltd. Reprinted by permission of the author.

Muriel Grainger: 'Love among the Ruins of London' from *Music at Midnight*, published 1950 by Fortune Press. Reprinted by permission of the author and Charles Skilton Ltd.

Joyce Grenfell: 'March Day, 1941' from *Poems by Contemporary Women*, edited by Theodora Roscoe and Mary Winter Were, published 1944 by Hutchinson & Co. Ltd. Reprinted by permission of Reginald P. Grenfell and Hutchinson Publishing Group Ltd.

Mary Hacker: 'Achtung! Achtung!' from *The Times Literary Supplement*, 13 October 1961. Reprinted by permission of the author and *The Times Literary Supplement*.

Gladys M. Haines: 'In War' from *Pines on the Hill*, published 1948 by Hutchinson & Co. Ltd. Reprinted by permission of Hutchinson Publishing Group Ltd.

Agnes Grozier Herbertson: 'Lament for a Cornish Soldier' from *Here Is My Signature*, published 1947 by Hutchinson & Co. Ltd. Reprinted by permission of Hutchinson Publishing Group Ltd.

Phoebe Hesketh: 'Spring in Wartime' and 'Post-War Christmas' from *Lean Forward, Spring*, published 1948 by Sidgwick & Jackson Ltd. Reprinted by permission of the author.

Molly Holden: 'Seaman, 1941' from *Air and Chill Earth*, published 1971 by Chatto & Windus Ltd. Reprinted by permission of Alan Holden and Chatto & Windus Ltd.

Pamela Holmes: 'Parting in April' from *Country Life*, April 1981. 'Missing, Presumed Killed' and 'War Baby' from the *Sunday Times*. Reprinted by permission of the author.

Libby Houston: 'Post-War' from *A Stained Glass Raree Show*, published 1967 by Allison & Busby Ltd. Reprinted by permission of the author and Allison & Busby Ltd.

Ada Jackson: 'Blessed Event' from *Poems by Contemporary Women*, edited by Theodora Roscoe and Mary Winter Were, published 1944 by Hutchinson & Co. Ltd. Reprinted by permission of Hutchinson Publishing Group Ltd.

Diana James: 'The Munition Workers' from *The Tune of Flutes*, published 1945 by George Routledge & Sons Ltd. Reprinted by permission of Routledge & Kegan Paul plc.

Wrenne Jarman: 'It Happened Before' from *The Breathless Kingdom*, published 1948 by Fortune Press. Reprinted by permission of Charles Skilton Ltd. 'The Neutral' from *Poems of This War by Younger Poets*, edited by Patricia Ledward and Colin Strang, published 1942 by Cambridge University Press. 'Plastic Airman' from *The Distaff Muse*, edited by Clifford Bax and Meum Stewart, published 1949 by Hollis & Carter Ltd. 'Threnody for Berlin – 1945' from *Nymph in Thy Orisons*, published 1960 by St Albert's Press.

F. Tennyson Jesse: 'Note to Isolationists 1940' from *The Compass*, printed 1951 for private circulation. Reprinted by permission of The Public Trustee, The Harwood Will Trust.

Lotte Kramer: 'Cissie' from *Contemporary Review*, 1974. 'Scrolls' from *A Lifelong House*, published 1983 by Hippopotamus Press. Reprinted by permission of the author.

Carla Lanyon Lanyon: 'Crusade in Europe' from *Selected Poems*, published 1954 by Guild Press.

Freda Laughton: 'The Evacuees' from *A Transitory House*, published 1945 by Jonathan Cape Ltd. Reprinted by permission of the author.

Margery Lawrence: 'Garden in the Sky' from *Fourteen to Forty-Eight*, published 1950 by Robert Hale Ltd. Reprinted by permission of Laurence Pollinger Ltd for the Estate of Margery Lawrence.

Margery Lea: 'Bomb Story (Manchester, 1942)' from *These Days*, published 1969 by Wilding & Son Ltd. Reprinted by permission of the author.

Patricia Ledward: 'Air-Raid Casualties: Ashridge Hospital' from *Poems of This War by Younger Poets*, edited by Patricia Ledward and Colin Strang, published 1942 by Cambridge University Press.

'Evening in Camp' from *I Burn for England*, edited by Charles Hamblett, published 1966 by Leslie Frewin Ltd.

Eiluned Lewis: 'The Children's Party' from *Morning Songs*, published 1944 by Macmillan & Co. Ltd. Reprinted by permission of The Society of Authors as the Literary Representative of the Estate of Eiluned Lewis.

Sylvia Lynd: 'Migrants' and 'The Searchlights' from *Collected Poems*, published 1945 by Macmillan & Co. Ltd. Reprinted by permission of the Literary Executors of the Estate of Sylvia Lynd.

Lilian Bowes Lyon: 'A Son' from *Tomorrow Is a Revealing*, published 1941 by Jonathan Cape Ltd. Reprinted by permission of the Executors of the Lilian Bowes Lyon Estate.

Prudence Macdonald: 'Spring 1940' and 'After Alamein' from *No Wasted Hour*, published 1945 by Sidgwick & Jackson Ltd.

Ethel Mannin: 'Song of the Bomber' from *Verse of Valour*, selected by John L. Hardie, published 1943 by Art & Educational Publishers Ltd. Reprinted by permission of the author.

Erica Marx: 'No Need for Nuremberg' and 'To One Put to Death in a Gas Chamber' from *Some Poems*, published 1955 by The Hand and Flower Press.

Frances Mayo: 'Lament' from *New Lyrical Ballads*, edited by Maurice Carpenter, Jack Lindsay and Heather Arundel, published 1945 by Editions Poetry London.

Naomi Mitchison: 'The Farm Woman: 1942' and '1943' from *The Cleansing of the Knives*, published 1978 by Canongate Publishing Ltd. Reprinted by permission of the author.

May Morton: 'To a Barrage Balloon' from *Sung to the Spinning Wheel*, published 1952 by Quota Press.

M. H. Noël-Paton: 'War Widow' from *Choose Something Like a Star*, printed 1972 for private circulation. Reprinted by permission of the author.

Evangeline Paterson: 'Female War Criminal' from *Whitelight*, published 1978 by Mid-Day Publications Ltd. 'History Teacher in the Warsaw Ghetto Rising' from *Bringing the Water Hyacinth to Africa*, published 1983 by Taxus Press. 'Poem for Putzi Hanfstaengel'. Reprinted by permission of the author.

Edith Pickthall: 'Evacuee' from *The Quest for Peace*, published

1963 by Outposts Publications. Reprinted by permission of the author.

Cecily Pile: 'With the Guerillas' and 'All Clear'. Previously unpublished. Printed by permission of the author.

Ruth Pitter: 'To a Lady, in a Wartime Queue' and 'Victory Bonfire' from *End of Drought*, published 1975 by Barrie & Jenkins Ltd. Reprinted by permission of Hutchinson Publishing Group Ltd.

Nancy Price: 'Take a Gun' from *Hurdy-Gurdy*, published 1944 by Frederick Muller Ltd.

Ida Procter: 'The One' from *War Poems from the 'Sunday Times'*, printed 1945 for private circulation.

Sylvia Read: 'For the War-Children' from *I Burn for England*, edited by Charles Hamblett, published 1966 by Leslie Frewin Ltd. Reprinted by permission of the author.

Anne Ridler: 'Now as Then', 'At Parting' and 'Before Sleep' from *The Nine Bright Shiners*, published 1943 by Faber & Faber Ltd. Reprinted by permission of the author.

Patricia M. Saunders: 'One of Our Aircraft Failed to Return' and '20th Century Requiem' from *Arena*, published 1948 by Hutchinson & Co. Ltd. Reprinted by permission of Hutchinson Publishing Group Ltd.

Myra Schneider: 'Drawing a Banana' from *Pick 7/8*, Summer 1977. Reprinted by permission of the author.

E. J. Scovell: 'Days Drawing In' from 'The First Year' in *Shadows of Chrysanthemums*, published 1944 by George Routledge & Sons Ltd. 'A Wartime Story' from *The Midsummer Meadow*, published 1946 by George Routledge & Sons Ltd. Reprinted by permission of the author.

Sheila Shannon: 'On a Child Asleep in a Tube Shelter' from *The Lightning-Struck Tower*, published 1947 by Frederick Muller Ltd. Reprinted by permission of the author.

Edith Sitwell: 'Still Falls the Rain' from *Collected Poems*, published 1957 by Macmillan & Co. Ltd. Reprinted by permission of David Higham Associates Ltd for the Estate of Edith Sitwell.

Margery Smith: 'For Freda' from *In Our Time*, published 1941 by Favil Press. 'The Unknown Warrior Speaks' from *Poems of*

This War by Younger Poets, edited by Patricia Ledward and Colin Strang, published 1942 by Cambridge University Press. Reprinted by permission of the author.

Stevie Smith: 'Voices against England in the Night' from *The Collected Poems of Stevie Smith*, published 1975 by Allen Lane Ltd. Reprinted by permission of James MacGibbon, Literary Executor of the Estate of Stevie Smith.

Sarah Stafford: 'The Unborn' from *I Burn for England*, edited by Charles Hamblett, published 1966 by Leslie Frewin Ltd.

Ruth Tomalin: 'Invasion Spring' from *Threnody for Dormice*, published 1947 by Fortune Press. Reprinted by permission of the author and Charles Skilton Ltd.

Catherine Brewster Toosey: 'Colour Symphony' from *Colour Symphony*, published 1941 by Grey Walls Press.

Margaret Wainwright: 'O Susanna' from *All the Quiet People*, published 1970 by Outposts Publications. Reprinted by permission of Outposts Publications and the author.

Sylvia Townsend Warner: 'Road 1940' from *Poems for France*, edited by Nancy Cunard, published 1944 by La France Libre. Reprinted by permission of Susanna Pinney, Literary Executor of the Estate of Sylvia Townsend Warner.

Dorothy Wellesley: 'Milk Boy' from *Selected Poems*, published 1949 by Williams & Norgate Ltd. 'Spring in the Park' from *The Poets*, published 1943 by H. W. Baldwin Ltd. Reprinted by permission of the Literary Executors of the Estate of Dorothy Wellesley.

Ursula Vaughan Williams: 'Penelope' from *Need for Speech*, published 1948 by Basil Blackwell Ltd. Reprinted by permission of the author.

Mary Wilson: 'Oxford in Wartime' from *New Poems*, published 1979 by Hutchinson. Reprinted by permission of the author and Hutchinson Publishing Group Ltd.

Diana Witherby: 'Casualty' from *Poems from 'New Writing'*, edited by John Lehmann, published 1946 by John Lehmann Ltd. Reprinted by permission of the author.

Elizabeth Wyse: extract from *Auschwitz: A Long Poem*, published 1974 by Taurus Press. Reprinted by permission of the author.

Biographical Notes

Biographical information has been supplied where possible, though in some cases it is incomplete.

VALENTINE ACKLAND (1906–69). Educated at Queen's College, London, and in Paris. A close friend of Sylvia Townsend Warner, with whom she published a collection of poems in 1933. During the war she served as a Civil Defence clerk in Dorset. She was converted to Roman Catholicism in 1946.

MABEL ESTHER ALLAN (b. 1915). Born in Wallasey, Cheshire. Educated at private schools. She served part of the war in the Women's Land Army in Cheshire, later becoming warden of a nursery attached to a Liverpool slum school. Author of many novels for children and young people, including four set in the Second World War. Lives in Heswall, Wirral.

PHYLLIS SHAND ALLFREY (1915–86). Born in Dominica, West Indies, where her father was Crown Attorney. During the war she returned to England, working for the London County Council as a welfare adviser to the bombed. A founder of the Dominican Labour Party, she was elected a federal Member of Parliament and made a Minister of the Federal Government. She was editor of the *Dominica Star*. A novelist and poet, her novel *The Orchid House* is reprinted in the Virago Modern Classics series.

LILIAN M. ANDERSON. Born in Norfolk. Educated at St Mary's Priory, Torquay. Married a Mr Robertson and lived in Axminster, Devon.

MARY DÉSIRÉE ANDERSON (1902–73). Born in Great Shelford, Cambridgeshire, daughter of Sir Hugh Anderson, Master of Gonville and Caius College, Cambridge. In 1936 she married Sir Trenchard Cox, who later became Director of the Victoria & Albert Museum. Lived in London throughout the war, publishing *British Women at War* in 1941.

JULIETTE DE BAIRACLI-LEVY. Born in Manchester of an Egyptian-born mother and a Turkish-born father. Educated at Withington Girls' High School, Manchester, and Lowther College, north Wales. She studied biology and veterinary medicine at Manchester and Liverpool universities but never formally qualified. During the war she worked in the Forestry Section of the Women's Land Army. Her brother and her childhood love were lost in the fighting, and relatives from France perished in the Nazi holocaust. Writer on herbal medicine. Settled on the island of Kythera, Greece.

JOAN BARTON (b. 1908). Born in Bristol, educated at Colston's Girls' School and Bristol University. When illness curtailed her studies she began her working life as a bookseller. Later she was employed by the BBC and by the British Council, where she directed a department during the war. In 1947 she and her partner, Barbara Watson, started the White House Bookshop in Marlborough, Wiltshire. Sold it after twenty years in business, moving to Salisbury.

JOYCE BARTON (b. 1915). An orphan of the First World War. As a teacher in Ipswich at the outbreak of war in 1939, she recalls controlling classes of more than forty children in unlit, unheated, earth-walled shelters while the German bombers flew overhead to London and back. She also remembers counting the squadrons of Spitfires going out and their depleted numbers returning. Married an army corporal who was later commissioned a captain. After the birth of her children she taught for fourteen years in Africa, then another seventeen in England before retiring in 1980. Lived in Ipswich.

RACHAEL BATES. Her poetry collection *Songs from a Lake* was published by Hutchinson & Co. Ltd in 1947. She lived in Ambleside in the Lake District.

MARJORIE BATTCOCK. Born in Highgate, London, and educated at The Study, Wimbledon Common, and King's College, London. Librarian, journalist and short-story writer. She was on fire-watching duty the night the first flying bomb reached London. From the roof of an office in Gower Street she saw it come down in flames at King's Cross, at that time believing it to be a German plane caught by anti-aircraft gunfire.

VERA BAX (1888–1974). Daughter of Colonel and Mrs Claude Rawnsley. First married to Stanley Kennedy North, artist and picture restorer. In 1918 she married Filson Young, who became editor of the *Saturday Review*. The two sons of this marriage were killed while flying on active service with the Royal Air Force, Pilot Officer Richard Filson Young in the Middle East, aged twenty-one, and Wing Commander William D. L. Filson Young in Burma, aged twenty-five. In 1927 she married Clifford Bax, the dramatist, poet and essayist. She painted in oils, specialising in portraiture, her work exhibited by the Royal Society of Portrait Painters. As a member of the Poets' Club she had many literary friends. The poems printed here are among several written during and after the war expressing her desolation in the loss of her sons.

MARY BEADNELL. Her poetry collection *Dale's Feet* was published by Outposts Publications in 1969. She lived near Skipton, Yorkshire.

AUDREY BEECHAM (1915–89). Educated at Wycombe Abbey School, and Somerville College, Oxford. She visited Spain briefly during the summer vacation of 1936, assisting the Catalonian anarchists. Engaged in freelance literary research work in London, 1938–40, then moved to Oxford, employed by the university in teaching and research, 1940–50. During the war years she was active in the Women's Home Defence, which was intended to support the Home Guard in the event of a German invasion. From 1950 to 1980 she continued an academic career at the University of Nottingham, spending the vacations in Oxford and retiring there.

MAUD ANNA BELL. Actively promoted the Serbian Relief Fund and other war charities during the First World War.

FRANCES BELLERBY (1899–1975). Born in Bristol of English and Welsh parentage, she attempted verse at the age of four. She was educated at Mortimer House, Clifton. Married John R. Bellerby. She lived for many years in Cornwall, then moved to Devonshire, to a house on the edge of Dartmoor. A novelist and short-story writer as well as a poet. Her work is largely concerned with the West Country, especially Cornwall.

ELIZABETH BERRIDGE. Spent the war years in London and in Wales, raising a family, writing, and helping her husband Reginald Moore (died 1990) to publish literary magazines, notably *Modern Reading*. His wartime correspondence with writers and publishers is now in the British Library. She has written nine novels, the latest being *Touch and Go*, 1995, and two collections of short stories. Four of her novels have been reissued in paperback, including *Across the Common*, winner of the Yorkshire Post Best Novel of the Year Award. Contributed to *The Daily Telegraph Book of Short Stories*, *New Writing 4*, and to BBC Radio 3 and 4; retired from a twenty-five-year stint of reviewing for the *Daily Telegraph*, 1990;

judge, David Higham First Novel Award, 1993–6.

MAJORIE BOULTON (b. 1924). Born in Teddington, Middlesex. Lived in Twickenham when very young but has spent a large part of her life in the north of England. Henry Treece as an English teacher helped her to go to Somerville College, Oxford, on scholarships. She became a teacher and principal of a college of education, returning to Oxford in 1971 to work for a doctorate. She now lives there as a full-time writer and is the author of *The Anatomy of Poetry* and other literary studies. Much of her creative work is done in the Esperanto language, in which she is internationally famous. A member of the Esperanto Academy, she has made numerous lecture tours abroad.

VERA BRITTAIN (1896–1970). Author, journalist and lecturer. Born in Newcastle-under-Lyme but spent her childhood in Macclesfield and Buxton. Educated at St Monica's, Kingswood, and Somerville College, Oxford, which she entered as an Exhibitioner in 1914. Abandoned Oxford temporarily to serve as a Voluntary Aid Detachment nurse during the war. Her experiences are recorded in *Testament of Youth*, first published in 1933 and a classic of its kind. At the end of the war, with all those closest to her dead, she returned to Oxford, where she met Winifred Holtby: this friendship continued and sustained her until the latter's untimely death in 1935. Vera Brittain wrote twenty-nine books in all. Married George E. G. Catlin, who was Professor of Politics at Cornell University. Their daughter is the politician Shirley Williams, Baroness Williams of Crosby.

ANNE BULLEY (b. 1922). Daughter of Ivo Bulley of St Edmund's School, Hindhead. Educated at St Swithun's, Winchester, and after the war at St Anne's, Oxford. She trained as a VAD; was employed in MI5; joined the Women's Royal Naval Service, serving in HMS *Mantis* in Lowestoft, HMS *Assegai* in Durban, and HMS *Highflyer* in Trincomalee, Ceylon (now Sri Lanka), from where she contributed to the Fleet Poetry Broadsheet. Later she became a potter; elected to the Art Worker's Guild, 1973. Now occupied in historical research, she published *Free Mariner* in 1992. Since 1948 has been married to Alan Maier; they have four children and twelve grandchildren.

MAY WEDDERBURN CANNAN (1893–1973). Poet and novelist.

Born in Oxford and educated at Wychwood School. Served in the Voluntary Aid Detachment and in the Intelligence Service during the war. Was engaged to Sir Arthur Quiller-Couch's son Bevil, who died of influenza shortly after the Armistice. Worked for the Oxford University Press in Oxford for some years and was Assistant Librarian at the Athenaeum Club, London. Married Brigadier P. J. Slater.

CHRISTINA CHAPIN. A schoolgirl poet of the First World War. Her collection *Poems, 1929–1941* was published by the Shakespeare Head Press in 1941.

SARAH CHURCHILL (1914–82). Daughter of Sir Winston and Lady Churchill. A dancer and actress, she first appeared on stage in 1936. Served in the Women's Royal Air Force as an aircraftwoman and subsequently as a commissioned officer from 1941 until 1945. Returning to the theatre, she concentrated on straight acting, appearing in the West End and touring Britain and the United States. Her writings include *A Thread in the Tapestry*, three volumes of poetry and her autobiography, *Keep on Dancing*. She was married three times, to Vic Oliver (marriage dissolved), Antony Beauchamp (died 1957) and Lord Audley (died 1963).

LOIS CLARK. Left school early to train at a college of dance and drama, where she worked with Karsavina for a while. She afterwards did some stage work, including television at the then very new Alexandra Palace. When war broke out she became an ambulance driver in her home town of Radlett, Hertfordshire, and volunteered for the Mechanised Transport Corps, which was providing women drivers for Civil Defence work in London. She drove a stretcher-party car during the Blitz in the Clapham and Brixton area, where there was plenty to be done in driving the first-aid parties, first on the scene at any bombing incident. On occasion she had to drive the mortuary van. Married in 1941 when her husband was serving in the forces.

ISABEL CONSTANCE CLARKE. Born in Plymouth and educated privately. Novelist, poet and biographer, writer of studies of Elizabeth Barrett Browning, Maria Edgeworth and the Brontës.

ALICE COATS (1905–78). Born in Birmingham, daughter of a Scottish clergyman. Educated at Edgbaston High School for Girls, Birmingham College of Art, the Slade School, London, and in Paris. Honorary Organising Secretary of the Birmingham Group of

Artists, 1933–9, she served in the Women's Land Army throughout the war. She acquired a high reputation for scholarship in garden history despite an increasing physical disability causing much pain. In recognition of her contribution to horticultural literature she was awarded the honorary degree of MA at Birmingham University and the Royal Horticultural Society's Veitch Memorial Medal. Lived in Handsworth, Birmingham.

DAME MARGARET POSTGATE COLE (1893–1980). Born in Cambridge, a professor's daughter. Educated at Roedean and Girton, she was for a short time classics mistress at St Paul's Girls' School before taking up political work in the Fabian Research Department in 1917. Married G. D. H. Cole, socialist writer, economist, labour historian and author. She wrote several books, some in collaboration with her husband – including many detective novels. She was Honorary Secretary of the Fabian Society from 1939, later becoming its President until her death, and also Chairman of the Further Education Committee of the London County Council in 1950, becoming an alderman in 1952.

MARION COLEMAN (b. 1898). Educated at Derby High School and Cheltenham Ladies' College. She studied medicine at the Royal Free Hospital, then worked as a general practitioner in several places including the East End of London and Hull. In 1944, having become a Roman Catholic, she joined the Catholic Committee for Relief Abroad and worked in a camp near Bari, southern Italy. Later she was attached to the Save the Children Fund in Germany and Poland. She became qualified in psychological medicine, working in Gloucester and London until retiring in 1975.

ELLODË COLLINS. Her poem 'Cessation of War' was first published in the *Spectator*. She lived in Bournemouth and London.

ALICE CORBIN (b. 1881). American. Born in St Louis. Was Associate Editor of the American publication *Poetry* from 1912 to 1916. Married a Mr Henderson and lived in Santa Fé, New Mexico.

FRANCES CORNFORD (1886–1960). Born in Cambridge, daughter of Sir Francis Darwin and granddaughter of Sir Charles Darwin. Educated at home. In 1909 she married Francis Macdonald Cornford, Fellow of Trinity College, Cambridge. They had five children, their eldest son being John Cornford, poet and communist activist, killed fighting for the Spanish republican cause in

December 1936. Apart from brief visits abroad, Frances Cornford lived in Cambridge all her life. During the war she was the centre of a lively household consisting of members of the family and refugees of various kinds. Part of her house was let to Dr Myer Salaman and his wife, Esther Polyanofsky. She collaborated with Esther Polyanofsky on *Poems from the Russian*, a volume of translations published by Faber in 1943.

NORAH K. CRUICKSHANK. Served in the Auxiliary Territorial Service and was attached to the Royal Army Service Corps. German scholar and translator.

NANCY CUNARD (1896–1965). Daughter of Sir Bache and Lady Cunard. After a disastrous marriage she settled in the Paris of the twenties and thirties in high café society and the world of jazz and Cubism. She was photographed by Cecil Beaton, painted by Kokoschka and Wyndham Lewis, and was re-created in novels by Ernest Hemingway and Aldous Huxley. At her home in Normandy she founded the Hours Press, issuing Samuel Beckett's first book and publishing the poems of Ezra Pound, Robert Graves and Richard Aldington. She compiled a negro anthology and celebrated its publication by joining the hunger marchers on the Great North Road in 1934. During the Spanish Civil War she went to Spain as correspondent for the *Manchester Guardian*. In the Second World War she worked for the Free French in London.

ELIZABETH DARYUSH (1887–1977). Born in London, daughter of Robert Bridges, the Poet Laureate. Educated by private tuition. She disowned her first three books of poems published in 1911, 1916 and 1921. Like her father she experimented with syllabics, although she still wrote in more orthodox metres. Her work has been compared with that of Thomas Hardy. She married Ali Akbar Daryush in 1923; lived for several years in Persia and finally at Boars Hill, Oxford.

EVA DOBELL (1867–1963). Daughter of Clarence Dobell, the Cheltenham wine merchant and local historian, and niece of the poet Sydney Dobell. Deeply distressed by the suffering and loss of life in the war, she volunteered as a nurse, and also took part in the morale-boosting work of corresponding with prisoners of war. Most of her life was spent in the Cotswolds, but she travelled extensively in Europe and north Africa. She helped and encouraged young poets, and campaigned in print for the protection of wildlife and the countryside.

HELEN PARRY EDEN (b. 1885). Born in London, lived in Enstone, Oxford and Woodstock. Educated at Roedean, Manchester University and King's College Art School. Contributed verse to *Punch*, *Pall Mall Magazine*, *The Catholic Messenger* and other journals. Was a Tertiary of the Servite Order.

BARBARA CATHERINE EDWARDS. Her collection *Poems from Hospital* was published by Outposts Publications in 1962.

GABRIELLE ELLIOT. American. Wrote for war organizations such as the American Fund for French Wounded, the Nursing Committee of the Council of National Defense, etc.

RUTH EVANS. Her poem 'A Roman in Libya' was first published in the *Sunday Times* then selected for the anthology *War Poems from the 'Sunday Times'*, printed for private circulation in 1945.

ELEANOR FARJEON (1881–1965). Born in London. Educated privately. She wrote fantasies and children's stories, and was one of those rare authors whose books find a devoted audience among both children and grown-ups. There is a Farjeon award for outstanding work in children's literature. She lived in Sussex and was a friend of the poet Edward Thomas and his wife, Helen. She became a Roman Catholic in 1951.

ELAINE FEINSTEIN (b. 1930). Born in Bootle, Lancashire, of Russian Jewish descent, and brought up in Leicester. Educated at Newnham College, Cambridge, later reading for the Bar. She married Dr Arnold Feinstein, a biochemist, in 1956. A prolific author of novels, short stories, translations and biographies, she has won several awards, grants and prizes; Fellow of the Royal Society of Literature, 1980. She lives and works in Cambridge.

MABEL FERRETT. Born in Yorkshire. She trained for teaching at Ripon Training College and taught at Armley National Boys' School, Leeds. The school was evacuated to Lincoln on 1 September 1939, eventually returning to Leeds and re-opening with a depleted staff so that she often had to cope with classes of sixty or even eighty children. Drafted into Civil Defence, she became a fire-watcher. She lives in Heckmondwike, West Yorkshire, and has worked for Kirklees Museums Service. Author of *The Brontës in the Spen Valley*, 1978, revised 1997, *The Taylors of the Red House*,

1987, and a novel, *The Angry Men*, twice broadcast on Radio 4, in 1967 and 1968. Salzburg University published her poetry collection *Scathed* in its series Salzburg Studies in English Literature, 1996.

OLIVIA FITZROY (1921–69). Born in Christchurch, Hampshire, daughter of Captain the Hon. R. O. FitzRoy, now Viscount Daventry. Educated at home by a governess, and from early childhood wrote prolifically. At the beginning of the war she worked in the library of a large London store, then joined the Women's Royal Naval Service. Serving as a flight direction officer, she was stationed at Yeovilton and later in Ceylon (now Sri Lanka). Her pilot boyfriend was killed near Singapore early in 1945. After the war she travelled with Chipperfield's Circus from 1947 until 1950, collecting material for a book. In 1951 she rented a croft in the Highlands of Scotland and lived there for almost five years. Married Sir Geoffrey Bates in 1957 and had two daughters. She published nine books, including the official history of the VIIIth King's Royal Irish Hussars, 1927–58.

S. GERTRUDE FORD. Worked for the 'women's cause' and appeared to be an ardent feminist. Contributed to *Poetry*, *Poetry Review* and other periodicals. Wrote *Lessons in Verse-craft*, published in London by C. W. Daniel, and edited thirty of the 'Little Books of Georgian Verse' for Erskine Macdonald.

KAREN GERSHON (1923–93). Born in Bielefeld, Germany, coming to England in 1938 with a refugee children's transport from Germany, where both her parents later died in concentration camps. She began writing poetry in English in 1950. Lived with her family of four children in Jerusalem from 1969 to 1973. Recipient of an Arts Council Poetry Award, the *Jewish Chronicle* Book Prize and a grant from the President of Israel, all awarded in 1967, and the Pioneer Women Poetry Award in 1968. She published several poetry collections, novels and non-fiction works. Lived in St Austell, Cornwall.

BEATRICE R. GIBBS (b. 1894). Born in Stoodley, Devon. Educated at St Margaret's School, Exeter, and Sherborne School for Girls, she became Co-Principal of Somerville School, St Leonards, Sussex. Short-story writer, poet, journalist, and writer of stories for children. She married J. H. G. Gibbs and lived latterly in Eastbourne.

VIRGINA GRAHAM (1910–92). Daughter of the well-known lyricist Harry Graham. Educated at Notting Hill High School and privately. Married Anthony Thesiger. Throughout the war she worked full-time with the Women's Voluntary Service. A contributor to many periodicals, including *Punch*, she was film critic for the *Spectator* from 1946 to 1956. A close friend of the late Joyce Grenfell.

MURIEL GRAINGER (b. 1905). Educated at South Hampstead High School. Writer and managing editor of a group of women's publications, now retired. Her entire war was spent in the neighbourhood of Fleet Street, keeping the magazines going. This work was regarded as important for morale and propaganda and was therefore a reserved occupation. A contributor to many periodicals and anthologies, she now lives in Hampstead Garden Suburb, London.

JOYCE GRENFELL (1910–79). Born in London; her mother was the sister of Nancy, Lady Astor. Educated at Claremont, Esher, Surrey. Married Reginald P. Grenfell in 1929. Actress and writer, she was radio critic for the *Observer*, 1936–9. During the war she appeared in Herbert Farjeon's revues and was a welfare officer in the Canadian Red Cross. She entertained troops in hospitals in Algiers, Malta, Sicily, Italy, Egypt, India and elsewhere. After the war she appeared in films, on television, and on stage in plays and concert shows, a much-loved entertainer who made many stage tours world-wide.

MARY HACKER (1908–95). Born in London. Novelist, poet and a contributor to several periodicals. She was married, had two sons and a daughter, and farmed near Harpenden, Hertfordshire. She wrote in 1984: 'I passed the 1914–18 war in north London being bombed while my mother tried to give me a normal life. I passed the war of 1939–45 also being bombed (luckily inaccurately) in north London, trying to give my children a reasonably normal life.'

GLADYS M. HAINES (b. 1904). Born in Dorset. In 1923 her family moved to the New Forest, where her father created a small nature sanctuary at Linwood. Her parents knew Thomas Hardy slightly through their friendship with Herman Lea, who wrote the first book on Hardy, and she remembers as a child being brought in to shake hands with the distinguished writer. During the war she worked in London as a clerk in the War Office, and experienced the air raids. After a period of office work in Birmingham she eventually retired to the family home in the New Forest.

CICELY HAMILTON (1872–1952). Born in London. Educated at private schools in England and Germany. She was a familiar figure on Suffragette platforms. During the First World War she served in a British women's hospital in France. Worked as a journalist and actress, and was also a playwright. Wrote *The Old Vic* (1926) in collaboration with Lilian Baylis, and *Marriage as a Trade*. Won the Femina Vie Heureuse prize for her short novel *William – an Englishman*. She was awarded a Civil List pension in 1938.

HELEN HAMILTON. Schoolteacher. Enjoyed rock-climbing and published *Mountain Madness* (1922) about her climbing experiences in the Alps.

ADA MAY HARRISON (1899–1958). Born in Port Elizabeth, South Africa. Educated there at East London High School, then at St Paul's Girls' School, London, and Newnham College, Cambridge. She held the Gilchrist Scholarship of the British School in Rome, 1922. In 1924 she married the painter Robert Austin, who illustrated most of her books. Author of *Some Tuscan Cities, Some Umbrian Cities*, novels, books for children, and joint author of a biography of Anne Brontë.

AGNES GROZIER HERBERTSON. Born in Oslo, Norway, she was educated privately. Novelist, short-story writer, poet, playwright, and writer for children. She lived in Liskeard, Cornwall.

PHOEBE HESKETH (b. 1909). Born in Preston, Lancashire. Educated in Southport and at Cheltenham Ladies' College. Journalist, scriptwriter for the BBC, and contributor to many periodicals. During the Second World War she was women's page editor of the *Bolton Evening News* but still found time to take in evacuees and do some Women's Voluntary Service work. Taught general studies at the Women's College, Bolton, 1967–9, and creative writing at Bolton School, 1976–8. On the Arts Council panels for *Poets Reading Poems* and *Poets in Schools*. She has published nine volumes of poetry and two of prose, and was awarded the Greenwood Prize of the Poetry Society in 1947 and 1966. Lives in Chorley, Lancashire.

MOLLY HOLDEN (1927–81). Born in London; her grandfather was the novelist Henry Gilbert. Educated at Commonweal Grammar School, Swindon, and King's College, London. She was married to Alan Holden, a schoolmaster, and had a son and a daughter. Novelist, poet, and writer of children's fiction, she received an Arts Council Award in 1971 and a Cholmondeley Award for poetry in 1972. Lived in Bromsgrove, Worcestershire.

PAMELA HOLMES. Educated at Benenden School. She was first married to Lieutenant F. C. Hall of the Rifle Brigade, who was attached to the East Surreys fighting in north Africa. He was posted missing, presumed killed, in December 1942. The poems 'War Baby' and 'Missing, Presumed Killed' were written directly from this experience when the author was twenty, and were published under the name 'Pamela Hall'. Their daughter was born four months after his death. Pamela Holmes has contributed poetry to various magazines and writes regularly for children. She lives in West Hythe, Kent. Mother of the distinguished biographer Richard Holmes.

TERESA HOOLEY (1889–1973). Born at Risley Lodge, Derbyshire. Educated by private governess, then at Howard College, Bedford.

LIBBY HOUSTON (b. 1941). Born in north London. Her father A. M. Houston, RAFVR bomber navigator, was posted missing, presumed dead, in 1943. She read English at Oxford University, and from American Beat-style readings in 1961 poetry became her main occupation, with years of performances, radio scripts, workshops and tutoring. Her books include *At the Mercy*, 1981, and *Necessity*, 1988. *All Change* (radio poems for children) was published by Oxford University Press in 1993. She was married to artist Mal Dean (died 1974) and has two children. Lives in Bristol, and works as a climbing botanist in the Avon Gorge.

ADA JACKSON. Born in Warwickshire. Her work was published in both Britain and the United States. E. V. Lucas named her 'the English Emily Dickinson', while in America she was called 'the Elizabeth Barrett Browning of our time'. She lived in Staffordshire.

DIANA JAMES (b. 1926). Born in London, and educated privately. Her verse was published in the *Spectator* when she was only fifteen and sixteen years of age. In 1953 she married Peter Gunn, a writer. Under the name Elizabeth Gunn she has written novels and other works, including a biography of Dorothy Wordsworth; a contributor to *New Statesman*, *Encounter* and other periodicals. Her novel *Ella's Dream* won a literary award from Yorkshire Northern Arts, 1971.

WRENNE JARMAN (d. 1953). Great-granddaughter of the poet Robert Millhouse, whose statue stands in Nottingham Castle. During the war she worked on a lathe at the Hawker Aircraft Works in Kingston, Surrey. She lived in Richmond, belonged to the Poets' Club and acted as hostess at literary gatherings in her home, when such prominent poets as Dylan Thomas would be invited to give readings. She became editor of the *Kensington News*.

ELINOR JENKINS. Some of her verse appeared in anthologies of the First World War period. A new edition of her *Poems*, published by Sidgwick & Jackson in 1921, included 'Last poems', implying that she had died c. 1920.

FRYNIWYD TENNYSON JESSE (1888–1958). Born in Chislehurst, Kent, daughter of the Rev. Eustace Tennyson d'Eyncourt Jesse, a nephew of Alfred, Lord Tennyson. She studied art at the Newlyn School in Cornwall, then in 1911 began a career as a journalist, writing for *The Times* and the *Daily Mail*. When war came she was one of the few women journalists to report from the Front. In 1918 she married the playwright H. M. Harwood, with whom she collaborated on several plays. She published nine novels, three collections of short stories and seven plays of her own, as well as poems and *belles-lettres*, and edited six volumes in the Notable British Trials series. Several of her novels are published in the Virago Modern Classics series.

ANNA GORDON KEOWN (1899–1957). Born in London. Educated at Cheltenham Ladies' College and in Dresden and Ireland. Married Philip Gosse. A novelist and poet; the foreword to her *Collected Poems* (Caravel Press, 1953) was written by Siegfried Sassoon.

LOTTE KRAMER. Jewish, born in Germany. She came to England in July 1939 as a refugee child with a children's transport organized by the Quakers. Her parents, family and friends were lost in the death camps. During the war she worked in a laundry. She studied art and history at evening classes while employed as a lady's companion and in a dress shop. Started to write poetry in 1970 and has published six collections, so far. The most recent are *The Desecration of Trees*, 1994, *Earthquake, and other poems*, 1994, and *Selected and New Poems 1980–1997*, 1997.

CARLA LANYON LANYON (1906–71). Born in County Down,

Northern Ireland. Her father was a flax broker and her mother the Irish poet Helen Lanyon. She married Brigadier Edward S. Hacker, MC. Poet, lecturer, poetry adjudicator, and contributor to anthologies and periodicals; her poems have also been recorded. She was winner of the Greenwood Prize of the Poetry Society, and the Farmer's Poetry International Award in Australia. She lived in Wiltshire and Surrey.

FREDA LAUGHTON (b. 1907). Born in Bristol and educated there. She was married twice, first to L. E. G. Laughton and then to John Midgley. Lived in Northern Ireland.

MARGERY LAWRENCE (1907–79). Born in Wolverhampton, she was educated privately at home and abroad. She published a book of verse at the age of sixteen and attended art schools in Birmingham, London and Paris. Married to Arthur E. Towle, she lived in Bryanston Place, Bloomsbury, and was a friend of Shane Leslie, Humbert Wolfe and other literary figures. Novelist, journalist and short-story writer.

MARGERY LEA (b. 1905). Educated at Elizabeth Gaskell College, Manchester, she worked as a schoolteacher in Buckinghamshire and Manchester, became a lecturer at Elizabeth Gaskell College, then Organizer and Inspector of Schools in Manchester. Her wartime duties included visiting Manchester evacuee children billeted in Shropshire, acting as liaison officer between the Education Authority and the reception area. She was involved in the Housewives' Education Campaign in Manchester, also in the plans for emergency feeding which were never needed. Retired to Shropshire.

PATRICIA LEDWARD (b. 1920). Educated at St Paul's Girls' School, she spent a year in Switzerland learning French. She had a job in Fleet Street during the Blitz of 1940–1, and later worked as a nurse in an emergency hospital. Joined the Auxiliary Territorial Service, spending three years as a driver with an anti-aircraft unit. Poet, novelist, anthologist and contibutor to many periodicals, she was co-editor of the anthology *Poems of This War by Younger Poets*, published by Cambridge University Press in 1942.

WINIFRED M. LETTS (1882–1971). Born in Ireland. Educated in Bromley. Served as Voluntary Aid Detachment nurse in 1915 at Manchester Base Hospital. Later joined the Almeric Paget Military

Massage Corps, working at Command Depot Camps in Manchester and Alnwick. Married W. H. Foster Verschoyle. Lived in Dublin in the 1930s, and in Faversham, Kent, in the 1940s.

EILUNED LEWIS (d. 1979). Born in Newtown, Montgomeryshire, Wales. Educated at Levana School, Wimbledon, and Westfield College, London. A journalist, she was on the editorial staff of the *Sunday Times*, 1931–6, and was a regular contributor to *Country Life*. In 1934 she was awarded the Book Guild Gold Medal. Married Graeme Hendry, a Scottish engineer, in 1937. Lived in Bletchingley, Surrey.

AMY LOWELL (1874–1925). American. Born in Brookline, Massachusetts, into the illustrious and wealthy New England family of Lowells. One of her brothers became President of Harvard, another was Percival Lowell the astronomer. She met Ezra Pound in England in 1913 and sought to influence the Imagist movement. Her quest for a hard-edged, unsentimental American verse was dubbed 'Amygism'. The posthumous edition of her *What's O'Clock* was awarded the Pulitzer Prize in 1925.

SYLVIA LYND (1888–1952). Born in Hampstead, London, daughter of A. R. Dryhurst of Dublin. Educated at King Alfred School, the Slade School and the Academy of Dramatic Art. Married Irish critic and essayist Robert Lynd in 1909. Member of the Femina Vie Heureuse Committee in 1923 and the Book Society Committee in 1929. A novelist, poet and short-story writer, she lived in London.

LILIAN BOWES LYON (1895–1949). Born in Bellingham, Northumberland, the youngest daughter of the Hon. Francis Bowes Lyon. A granddaughter of the 13th Earl of Strathmore and a cousin of Queen Elizabeth the Queen Mother. She worked in London and abroad, and on the land, with a particular devotion to the Northumbrian countryside. Although severely crippled during her last years, she volunteered to help victims of the bombing in the blitzed East End of London.

DAME ROSE MACAULAY (1889–1958). Born in Cambridge, daughter of G. C. Macaulay, a classical scholar and lecturer in the university. Went to school and college in Oxford, but spent most of her childhood in Italy. A prominent novelist, essayist and poet, she won several major literary prizes, including the Femina Vie

Heureuse and the James Tait Black Memorial Prize. Clever and critical, she belonged to the Bloomsbury Group. She was renowned for her enormous vigour and zest for life, which she retained even in old age.

PRUDENCE MACDONALD. Her poetry collection *No Wasted Hour* was published by Sidgwick & Jackson in 1945. She lived in Maidstone, Kent.

ETHEL MANNIN (1900–84). Born in London and educated at a local council school. She became editor of *The Pelican*, a theatrical newspaper, in 1918. A prolific novelist, biographer and travel writer, she joined the Independent Labour Party in 1932. She was married twice, to J. A Porteous in 1920 and Reginald Reynolds in 1938. Throughout the war she lived and worked in London. Lived in Teignmouth, Devon.

ERICA MARX (1909–67). Born in Streatham, London, daughter of a banker. She was educated at schools in England, Wales and France, and at King's College, London. From 1941 to 1943 she was Commandant of the Women's Home Defence in Surrey. To assist novice poets she founded the Hand and Flower Press in Ashford, Kent, publishing the Poems in Pamphlet paperback series. She was on the management board of the Poetry Book Society, 1953–7. Some of her work was written under the pseudonym 'Robert Manfred'.

FLORENCE RIPLEY MASTIN (b. 1896). American. Educated at Barnard College, Columbia University. Taught English and creative poetry at Erasmus Hall High School, Brooklyn, New York. A member of the Poetry Society of America and winner of poetry awards. Contributor to the *New York Times*, the *Saturday Review* and other periodicals.

FRANCES MAYO. Her poem 'Lament' was first published in the anthology *New Lyrical Ballads*, edited by Maurice Carpenter, Jack Lindsay and Honor Arundel, published by Editions Poetry London in 1945.

CHARLOTTE MEW (1869–1928). Born in Bloomsbury, daughter of an architect. Educated at the Lucy Harrison School for Girls Gower Street. Overwhelmed by ill-health, family deaths and poverty, she had a poor opinion of herself and her writing. Her output was small but extraordinary – so much so that she was awarded a Civil List pension on the recommendation of Thomas Hardy, John Masefield and Walter de la Mare. She was a petite, eccentric-looking woman, appearing in mannish clothes at Harold Monro's Poetry Bookshop where poets regularly met. She finally committed suicide.

ALICE MEYNELL (1847–1922). Born in Barnes but spent most of her childhood in Italy. Wife of Wilfred Meynell, the author and journalist, and mother of Everard, Francis and Viola. A poet and essayist, she was converted to Roman Catholicism in 1872 and carried her religious beliefs into her writing. While she was still a girl, her poems had been warmly praised by established writers. Her output of verse and prose was small but always fine in style and content. She and her husband were on intimate terms with the great literary figures of the time – Browning, Tennyson, Ruskin, Rossetti, Patmore, Meredith and George Eliot.

RUTH COMFORT MITCHELL (1882–1953). American. Born in San Francisco. Married William Sanborn Young.

NAOMI MITCHINSON (b. 1897). Born in Edinburgh, daughter of the physiologist J. S. Haldane. She married G. R. Mitchison in 1916. A feminist and socialist, she served on Argyll County Council for several periods between 1946 and 1965, and was a member of the Highland and Island Advisory Panel, 1947–65, and the Highlands and Islands Development Consultative Council, 1966–73. A prolific writer, recognized as an outstanding historical novelist, she was created a life peer in 1964 but prefers not to use the title. She has been tribal mother to the Bakgatla of Botswana since 1963. Her novel *The Corn King and the Spring Queen* is published in the Virago Modern Classics series. She has homes in London and Carradale, Scotland.

HARRIET MONROE (1861–1936). American. Born in Chicago. Educated at the Academy of the Visitation, Georgetown. She lectured on poetry and did some newspaper work, chiefly in literary criticism. Founder of *Poetry*, the first American periodical devoted exclusively to verse, and was its editor from 1912 to 1936.

MAY MORTON. Of Ulster. A schoolteacher, she retired in 1934. A contributor to various literary magazines and to BBC radio programmes in Northern Ireland.

EDITH NESBIT (1858–1924). Born in London. Educated at a

French convent. Spent her early youth in the country at Holstead Hall, Kent. She began her literary career by writing poetry but is best remembered for her children's stories. Married Hubert Bland in 1880. She took a keen interest in socialism, and in 1883 was one of the founders of the 'Fellowship of New Life' out of which, in 1884, sprang the Fabian Society. She was a woman of striking appearance and great personal charm.

MARGARET HAMILTON NOËL-PATON (b. 1896). Born in Bombay, India. Her grandfather was the Scottish artist Sir Joseph Noël-Paton. Formerly Girls' Work Secretary for the YWCA in India and Ceylon, she spent the war years in rural Somerset, where her cottage became a brief haven for exhausted wardens and fire-watchers from frequently bombed Cardiff and Bristol. She was a volunteer helper in several camps for displaced persons, mainly Serbs and Poles who would never be able to return to their homelands. She settled in Edinburgh.

HON. ELEANOUR NORTON (b. 1881). The twin daughter of John R. B. Norton, 5th Baron Grantley. She lived in London and at Markenfield Hall, Ripon, the family home in Yorkshire.

CAROLA OMAN (1897–1978). Born in Oxford, daughter of the historian Sir Charles Oman. Educated at Wychwood School, Oxford. Served as a nurse with the British Red Cross Society on the Western Front from 1916 to 1919. Married Sir Gerald Lenanton. A versatile writer of novels and historical biography, she was awarded the *Sunday Times* annual British literature prize for *Nelson* (1948) and the James Tait Black Memorial Prize for *Sir John Moore* (1953). A Trustee of the National Portrait Gallery, she was made Commander, Order of the British Empire in 1957.

MAY O'ROURKE (b. 1898). Born in Ballymena, then lived in Comber, near Belfast. Her father was a Supervisor of Inland Revenue in the Civil Service. The family eventually moved to London, then Dorset. Educated by the Sisters of Sainte Marie at Maumbury House. Became secretary to Thomas Hardy in March 1923, when she was twenty-five, and was the friend and confidante of both Hardy and his wife Florence.

EVANGELINE PATERSON. Born in Limvady, Northern Ireland, brought up in Dublin. As a child she remembers feeling terrified at the news of the fall of France, expecting German soldiers to appear over the garden wall at any moment. She is married to a professor of geography, has three children, and has lived in Cambridge, St Andrews, Leicester and South Africa. Collections of her poetry have been published and she has won prizes in national competitions. *Lucifer and the Fair* was nominated for a Forward Poetry Prize, 1992.

EDITH PICKTHALL (b. 1893). Educated at a private school in Oxton, Birkenhead, Cheshire. She worked in a Liverpool office, then trained as a maternity nurse and midwife before moving to Mylor, near Falmouth, Cornwall, as housekeeper to relatives, in 1938. Mylor was a reception area for evacuees. She joined the village Red Cross Detachment, which had established a first-aid post, and attended to the ailments of the evacuees, principally impetigo and nits. The village was bombed in 1941, resulting in some loss of life, one of the casualties being a small evacuee. Acting as an emergency midwife during most of the war, on one late-night call she had to take cover from a low-flying enemy plane that was firing indiscriminately over the district.

CECILY PILE (b. 1914). Born in Stanmore, Middlesex. She worked for forty years at the head office of the Milk Marketing Board, for twenty years as Librarian. During the war her job was classed as a reserved occupation so her wartime experience was as a civilian dodging the air raids and singing with the Morley College Choir. She now lives in Devon.

RUTH PITTER (1897–1992). Born in Ilford, Essex. Educated at Coburn School for Girls, Bow, East London. During the First World War she was a clerk in the War Office. She worked as a painter for the Walberswick Peasant Pottery Company in Suffolk from 1918 to 1930. A poet of distinction, she won the Hawthornden Prize, the Heinemann Foundation Award, and the Queen's Medal for Poetry. She was created a Companion of Literature in 1974. She lived near Aylesbury, Buckinghamshire.

JESSIE POPE (d. 1941). Born in Leicester. Educated at Craven House, Leicester, and North London Collegiate School. Contributed some 200 poems and articles to *Punch*. Wrote humourous fiction, verse and articles for leading popular magazines and newspapers. Married Edward Babington Lenton. Lived in Fritton near Great Yarmouth.

NANCY PRICE (1880–1970). Educated at Malvern Wells,

Worcestershire. A distinguished actress, she first went on stage in 1889, playing more than four hundred parts during her career. In 1907 she married Colonel Charles R. Maude. She became a producer, with eighty-seven plays to her credit, and was appointed an Honorary Director of the People's National Theatre in 1933. A writer on nature and the countryside, she lived at High Salvington, Sussex.

IDA PROCTER. Born in London. She studied book-illustration at Kingston School of Art in Surrey. During the Second World War she worked as a draughtswoman in a firm of precision engineers. After the war she married David Fraser Harris. In 1954 they moved to Cornwall, where she still lives. Her books include *Masters of British Painting, Masters of Nineteenth-Century British Art* and *Visitors to Cornwall.* Some of her poetry was published in *The Sunday Times*, *Evening Standard*, etc. An occasional contributor to Cornish periodicals such as *Cornish Life*.

DOROTHY UNA RATCLIFFE (1894–1967). Born at Preston Park, Sussex. Educated privately and in Weimar and Paris. Author of many books of verse and prose. Also wrote peasant plays, devoting herself to the dialects of the Yorkshire Dales where she lived following her first marriage. She was Lady Mayoress of Leeds in 1914. A contributor to many North Country newspapers and magazines, she became President of the Yorkshire Dialect Society. A relative by marriage of the 1st Lord Brotherton, she gave his library to Leeds University and added liberal endowments from his large fortune. She married three times.

SYLVIA READ. Both a writer and an actress. Her poems have been published in many periodicals and broadcast on BBC radio and television. As a very young girl in wartime she gave performances of poetry to the Forces in Britain. She also worked as a leading actress with the Pilgrim Players under E. Martin Browne, touring camps and villages. Now works full-time with her husband William Fry for their two-person touring theatre known as Theatre Roundabout, which has performed all over Britain, the United States, Western Europe and in Africa. They have appeared in the West End and on television.

ANNE RIDLER (b. 1912). Born in Rugby, daughter of the poet H. C. Bradby, who was a housemaster at Rugby School. Educated at

Downe House School, King's College, London, and in Florence and Rome. She spent five years with the publishers Faber and Faber, working as an editorial assistant and as secretary to T. S. Eliot. Married Vivian Ridler, Printer to Oxford University, in 1938. Poet, librettist, editor and anthologist, she has also written several verse plays. Lives in Oxford.

URSULA ROBERTS (b. 1887). Born in Meerut, India. Educated in Highgate and at London University. A contributor to literary reviews and periodicals, she was a member of the Executive Anglican Group for Ordination of Women. Married the Rev. W. C. Roberts and lived in Woburn Square, WC1. Wrote under the name 'Susan Miles'.

LADY MARGARET SACKVILLE (1881–1963). Daughter of the 7th Earl de la Warr. She was mainly a poet, but wrote some books for children. Much of her life was spent in Edinburgh, although she lived in Cheltenham latterly.

PATRICIA M. SAUNDERS. Her poetry collection *Arena* was published by Hutchinson & Co. Ltd in 1948.

MYRA SCHNEIDER (b. 1936). Born in London but spent most of her early childhood and all the war years in Gourock on the Firth of Clyde. She studied English at London University and has lived in London ever since. When she was first married she taught at comprehensive schools in the East End, then later taught handicapped adults at a day centre in Colindale. Author of three collections of poetry, and books for children and teenagers. Now a freelance writer, she has contributed to many periodicals. Also writes under the name 'Sarah Grovelands'.

LADY AIMEE BYNG SCOTT (d. 1953). Daughter of General C. H. Hall, she married Major-General Sir Arthur Scott in 1894. She published a number of poems and plays, writing under the name 'Alec Holmes'.

E. J. SCOVELL (b. 1907). Born in Sheffield, Yorkshire. Educated at Casterton School, Westmorland, and Somerville College, Oxford. In 1937 she married an Oxford biologist, and they have children and grandchildren. Lives in Oxford and was there throughout the war. She has published seven volumes of poetry; a collected edition was published by Carcanet Press in 1988.

SHEILA SHANNON (b. 1913). Born in London and lived and worked there throughout the war. In 1946 she married the poet and broadcaster Patric Dickinson. They have a son and a daughter. She worked with W. J. Turner on the publication of the Britain in Pictures series, 1940–6. Co-editor with Turner of the anthologies *New Excursions into English Poetry* and with Patric Dickinson of *Poems to Remember* and *Poets' Choice*. She has reviewed poetry in the *Spectator*, contributed poems to many periodicals and was editor of *Great Lives,* Volume V of the *Oxford Junior Encyclopaedia*. Lives in Rye, Sussex.

MAY SINCLAIR (1865–1946). Born in Rock Ferry, Cheshire. Educated at Cheltenham Ladies' College. Served with the British Red Cross in a Field Ambulance Corps, Belgium, during the First World War. Her first short story was published in 1895 and her first novel in 1896. She also wrote on philosophical idealism. The best of her popular books were experimental in technique and based on the new Freudian psychology. In her time she was considered one of the greatest of the Georgian novelists, but her work met with far greater success in America than in Britain.

EDITH SITWELL (1887–1964). Born in Scarborough, sister of Osbert and Sacheverell, into an aristocratic family of wealth and culture. She rebelled at an early age against the social role expected of a young English girl of high birth. Recognized as one of the most eminent poets of her time, she received honorary degrees from the Universities of Leeds, Durham, Oxford, Sheffield and Hull. She became a Roman Catholic in 1954, the year she was made a Dame Commander, Order of the British Empire. Vice-President of the Royal Society of Literature in 1958.

CICILY FOX SMITH (d. 1954). Born in Lymm, Cheshire. Educated at Manchester High School for Girls. She contributed to many journals, her special subject being the history of the sea. Latterly lived in Sutton Scotney, Hampshire.

MARGERY SMITH (b. 1916). Poet, teacher, editor and secretary. She worked as a guide at Newstead Abbey, Nottinghamshire, 1940–2, and was co-founder of Nottingham Poetry Society. Served in the Auxiliary Territorial Service, 1942–6. During the war her poem 'The Unknown Warrior Speaks' was set to music for a male-voice choir by Kent Kennan and was performed at a concert in the White House, Washington. This poem was read in the D-Day concert 'We'll Meet Again', as broadcast in America on 6 June 1994. She taught in Romania in 1937 and in Iraq from 1950 to 1953. She has been a council member of the Poetry Society. With Hannah Kelly she edited the fifth and sixth anthologies of Camden Poetry Group, 1979 and 1982. Of her three poetry collections, the latest is *In Transit*, published by Outposts Publications in 1982. She lives in Horsham, Sussex.

STEVIE SMITH (1902–71). Born in Hull, Yorkshire, but lived at Palmers Green, north London, from the age of three. Educated at Palmers Green High School and North London Collegiate School for Girls. She worked as a secretary for publishers Sir Neville Pearson and Sir Frank Newnes until 1953. Poet and novelist known for her distinctive line drawings. An occasional writer and broadcaster for the BBC, she often read her poems with comments, sometimes singing them to her own music based largely on Gregorian chants and hymn tunes. She served on the Arts Council literary panel, and received the Cholmondeley Award in 1966 and the Queen's Gold Medal for Poetry in 1969.

SARAH STAFFORD. Her poem 'The Unborn' has been published in several anthologies. She lived in west London and taught English to Belgian children.

MARIE CARMICHAEL STOPES (1880–1958). The pioneer advocate of contraception, she was a Suffragette and palaeontologist. In 1904 she became the first female science lecturer at Manchester University. Her famous book *Married Love* sold millions of copies throughout the world. With her second husband, Humphrey Verdon Roe, the aircraft manufacturer, she founded the first birth-control clinic in north London in 1921. Throughout a turbulent life devoted to sex education she was involved in many legal battles. She kept every scrap of paper – a biographer's dream.

MURIEL STUART (d. 1967). Born in London. She wrote poetry from an early age, her first major work appearing in the *English Review* in 1916. She had encouragement from Thomas Hardy, who called her work 'superlatively good'. Two volumes of poetry were published in 1918 and a third in 1922, followed by an American edition in 1926. In a foreword to the American edition Henry

Savage wrote: 'Alice Meynell being dead, there is no English poet living today who is Muriel Stuart's peer.' With Mrs C. A. Dawson Scott, she was a founder member of the P.E.N. Club in 1921.

MILLICENT SUTHERLAND (1867–1955). Millicent Gower, Duchess of Sutherland. First daughter of 4th Earl of Rosslyn. Wrote a graphic account of her impressions of the German invasion of Belgium entitled *Six Weeks at the War*, published by *The Times* in 1914. Joined the French Red Cross and took the 'Millicent Sutherland Ambulance' to the front with a doctor and eight nurses. Received the French Croix de Guerre and the Belgian Red Cross 1st Class. Held the Queen's canopy at the coronation of George V. Sometime President of the Scottish Home Industries Association and the Potteries and Newcastle Cripples Guild.

SARA TEASDALE (1884–1933). American. Born in St Louis. Her poetry was much influenced by the work of Christina Rossetti. She was courted by Vachel Lindsay but eventually married a St Louis businessman. Her health failed, she took an overdose of sleeping medicine and was found drowned in her bath.

AELFRIDA TILLYARD (b. 1883). Born in Cambridge, sister of E. M. W. Tillyard, the eminent scholar and critic. Educated in Lausanne and at the University of Florence. Married Constantine Graham and lived in Oxford.

RUTH TOMALIN. Born in Piltown, Co. Kilkenny, Ireland. Educated at Chichester High School, Sussex, and King's College, London. She served in the Women's Land Army, 1941–2. A staff reporter on various newspapers, 1942–65, she became a freelance press reporter at London law courts in 1966. Novelist, poet, writer on natural history, biographer, and writer of children's stories.

CATHERINE BREWSTER TOOSEY (b. 1905). Born in the north of England. She lived in Canada for a time, returning to England during the war. Her short stories, articles and poems were published in British and American magazines, and in 1940 she won first prize in an American poetry competition. Encouraged by Walter de la Mare and Richard Church, she turned entirely to writing verse. Lived in Welwyn Garden City, Hertfordshire, and Guildford, Surrey.

IRIS TREE (1897–1968). Born in London, daughter of Herbert Beerbohm Tree, the famous actor-manager. Her first poems were published when she was sixteen. She studied art at the Slade and became popular with the Bloomsbury Group. She was married twice, first to American photographer Curtis Moffat, then to Count Friedrich Ledebur. A genuine Bohemian, an eccentric and a wit, original in all aspects of her life and character, she shared a secret studio in London with Nancy Cunard. She was photographed by Cecil Beaton and painted by Augustus John.

ALYS FANE TROTTER (1863–1962). English-born, she went to South Africa in the 1890s with her husband, who was employed by the Cape Colonial Government. Attracted by the beauty of old Cape Dutch houses, she wrote and illustrated *Old Cape Colony* (Constable, 1903). On her return to England she wrote poetry, often contributing to *Punch*, the *Cornhill Magazine* and other periodicals.

KATHARINE TYNAN (1861–1931). Born in Clondalkin, Co. Dublin, daughter of a farmer. A Roman Catholic, she was educated at Siena Convent, Drogheda, and began writing at the age of seventeen. During the war she did philanthropic work and some nursing, and had two sons serving in Palestine and France respectively. A poet and prose writer, she was a leading member of the Celtic literary revival and a friend of Yeats, Parnell, the Meynells and the Rossettis.

ALBERTA VICKRIDGE. Born in Bradford and educated at Bradford Girls' Grammar School. Served as a Voluntary Aid Detachment nurse in the war. Her recreations were printing, verse publishing and astronomy. In 1927 she founded the Jongleur Press and became its editor.

MARGARET WAINWRIGHT (b. 1927). Born in Bradford, Yorkshire, one of the three daughters of a painter and decorator who was very ambitious for his family. She was evacuated during the first year of war but soon returned home. In 1946 she went up to St Hilda's College, Oxford, with an Exhibition and a state supplementary scholarship. Between 1950 and 1970 her time was spent first in teaching, then as an editor with an educational publisher. In 1971 she married a trawlerman, and undertook several non-academic jobs including work in a factory and as a driver. Both she and her husband have published poetry booklets. She has written under her married name of Surtees.

SYLVIA TOWNSEND WARNER (1893–1978). Born in Harrow,

Middlesex, daughter of a housemaster at Harrow School. She received no formal education. During the First World War she worked in a munitions factory. A distinguished novelist, poet and short-story writer, she spent several years as co-editor of the Oxford University Press ten-volume work *Tudor Church Music*. Her 1967 biography of T. H. White was judged by the *Guardian* to be one of the outstanding biographies of the period. She received the Prix Menton in 1969. A close friend of T. F. Powys and Valentine Ackland, she lived latterly at Maiden Newton, Dorset.

MARY WEBB (1881–1927). Born in Leighton, near the Wrekin, Shropshire, daughter of a schoolmaster. Educated in Southport, she began writing verse at the age of ten, afterwards writing fairy tales. Married Henry B. L. Webb in 1912. She published verse and prose in various newspapers and magazines in Britain and America before moving to London in 1921, reviewing for *The Bookman* and other periodicals. Best known for her novels, which are set in the Welsh border country and portray shy heroines in scenes of rustic beauty. Her literary success dated from the occasion when her work was praised by Stanley Baldwin, then prime minister. She was awarded the Femina Vic Heureuse Prize for *Precious Bane*, the best English novel of 1924–5. Her novels are brilliantly satirized by Stella Gibbons in *Cold Comfort Farm*.

M. WINIFRED WEDGWOOD. Served with the Devonshire 26th Voluntary Aid Detachment.

DOROTHY WELLESLEY (1889–1956). Born at Croughton, Cheshire, daughter of Robert Ashton. Educated privately, she travelled widely. Married the Hon. Gerald Wellesley, who became the 7th Duke of Wellington. A frequent contributor to literary magazines and anthologies, she was editor of the Hogarth Living Poets series from 1928 to 1932.

CATHERINE DURNING WHETHAM. Lived in Ottery St Mary, Devonshire. Married Cecil Dampier and had six children – five girls and one boy. Wrote *The Upbringing of Daughters* (Longman, 1917).

LUCY WHITMELL. Her poem ‘Christ in Flanders’ was originally published in *The Spectator* on 11 September 1915 under the initials ‘L. W.’; it was reprinted widely and became one of the most popular and most anthologized poems of the war.

URSULA VAUGHAN WILLIAMS (b. 1911). Born in Malta. Educated privately in England and Brussels. Novelist, poet, biographer and librettist. She has been married twice, in 1933 to Michael Forrester Wood (died 1942) and in 1953 to the composer Ralph Vaughan Williams, OM (died 1958). She has written libretti for the operas and choral works of twenty-two composers, including Ralph Vaughan Williams, Anthony Milner, Elisabeth Lutyens, Roger Steptoe and Malcolm Williamson. Her earlier work was published under the name 'Ursula Wood'. She lives in London.

MARGARET ADELAIDE WILSON. American. Born in Erie, Pennsylvania, but lived for some time in California.

MARJORIE WILSON. Sister of the war poet Captain T. P. Cameron Wilson. Their father was the Rev. T. Cameron Wilson of Little Eaton, Derby. Her war work included service in the War Relief Office and Voluntary Aid Detachment nursing in Netley.

MARY WILSON. Born in Diss, Norfolk, daughter of the Rev. D. Baldwin, a Congregational Minister. Wife of the late Harold Wilson, former Labour prime minister, Lord Wilson of Rievaulx. Her childhood was spent in East Anglia and she began to write verse at the age of six. Three collections of her poetry have been published and she edited an anthology entitled *Poems I Like*, published by Hutchinson in 1982. She has two sons and twin granddaughters, and has homes in London and the Isles of Scilly.

DIANA WITHERBY (b. 1915). Born in London but much of her childhood was spent in the country. She returned to live in London and remained there throughout the war. She began writing reviews, short stories and poems, some of which were broadcast and others published in periodicals such as the *Listener* and *Penguin New Writing*. For a time she worked as reader for the wartime monthly literary magazine *Horizon*, in which many established and 'new' (now well-known) writers were published. Married Sir Samuel Cooke, who became a High Court judge, and by whom she has two sons. Her husband died in 1978 after thirty-five years of marriage. Her work was praised by Robert Graves.

ELIZABETH WYSE (b. 1957). Her long poem *Auschwitz*, part of which is reprinted here, was published in a limited edition by Taurus Press in 1974. She has lived and worked in France for several years.

Index of First Lines